I'VE JUST SEEN A PLACE I CAN'T FORGET

WALKING IN THE FOOTSTEPS OF THE BEATLES

COLIN UNWIN

Copyright © 2014 by Colin Unwin

All rights reserved.

No part of this book may be reproduced in any form or by any electronic or mechanical means including information storage and retrieval systems, without permission in writing from the author. The only exception is by a reviewer, who may quote short excerpts in a review.

Paperback ISBN – 978-1-910256-87-9

ACKNOWLEDGEMENTS

Many thanks to John Halliday for befriending me and making my passion for finding out more about four world famous lads from Liverpool even greater.

Thanks to my lovely wife Lynn, my son David and daughter Hayley and my two chickens, Luca and Nico, who have had to put up with Grandpops, The Beatlemaniac.

I love you always.

PROLOGUE

I was fourteen when I got a job in a garage. I was that passionate about pop music I was always getting in trouble for switching customers' car radios on, to listen to the latest songs.

For four years in the 1960s I went to the Oasis coffee bar in Manchester to listen to all the best bands and twice tried in vain to get in and listen to this up and coming group called The Beatles.

Forty years later I was overcome by a great passion to find out where in Liverpool's back streets those four lads grew up to become the biggest band in the world.

While wandering the streets of Liverpool over a period of seventeen years my interest in The Beatles was noticed by somebody who worked for the National Trust and who encouraged me to take over the tenure as custodian at the Trust's John Lennon and Paul McCartney childhood homes.

Some of the stories in this book are about The Beatles' places I discovered and some are about living in the two iconic pop stars homes and the strong feeling that John was there with me on one of the nights that I stayed in his Aunt Mimi's house.
    Then there's the reason why I had to paint Strawberry Field gates and why I needed to safely secure Stuart Sutcliffe's headstone back in the ground at Huyton cemetery.

Frustration was my only reward when I tried to have a plaque put up to commemorate the time and place where Beatlemania was born, only to have my request turned down.

In the last seventeen years I have travelled hundreds of miles around Liverpool, driving and walking down the back Streets that sang out to me, to find the places where John, Paul, George, Ringo and Stuart Sutcliffe lived there lives. This book records the stories I uncovered about them.

Contents

1 - Music, Music, Music   11
2 - Where In Liverpool Did Buddy Play?   17
3 - What Happened In Allerton Cemetery?   26
4 - Eleanor Whitefield   29
5 - Walk That Walk To John And Paul's   39
6 - The Door Opened To 20 Forthlin Road   44
7 - For The Benefit Of Who?   54
8 - A Lady, A Dog And Two Chinese Girls In The McCartney's Back Yard   58
9 - Walking Through Calderstone Park   63
10 - A Day To Remember In Mendips   72
11 - From Behind A Curtain   78
12 - The Teddy Boys Mean Trouble   82
13 - The Beatlemania Plaque That Never Was   93
14 - The Door Opens To Aunt Mimi's   96
15 - Sgt. Pepper Arrives At Mendips   105
16 - The Strawberry Field Gates Are Vandalised   111
17 - The Living Dream   117
18 - John Lost His Job And I Lost Mine   122

FOREWORD

This is the autobiography of Colin Unwin, a man with a Beatles obsession.

Unusually, it's a book about a man whose obsession with the Fab Four began as a result of an unsuccessful visit to a gig the group were playing in 1962, where he couldn't get in to see the up-and-coming but, then, largely unknown band from Liverpool.

Back then, where this story begins, the young Beatles' fan was a garage mechanic who would one day live and work in John Lennon and Paul McCartney's childhood homes and become well known as the man who rescued a treasured monument by repainting the famous Strawberry Field gates.

Colin finds Strawberry Field in 1992.

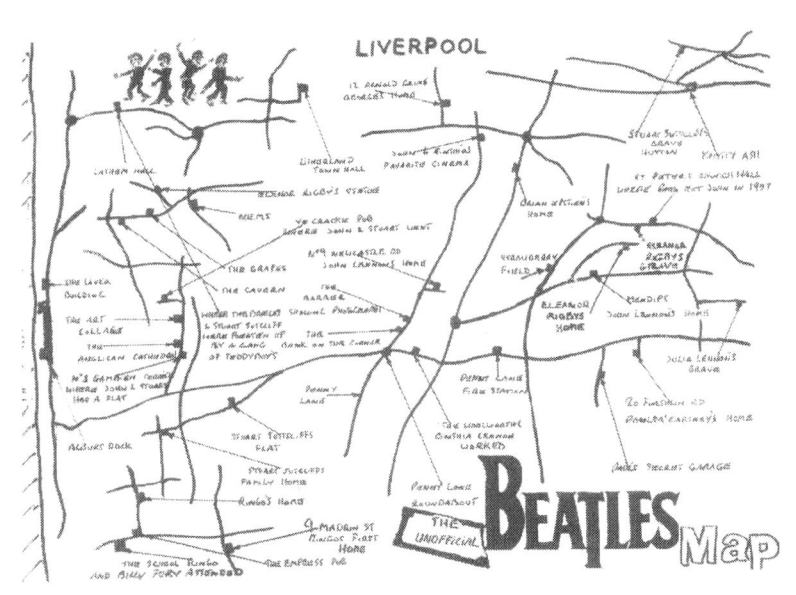

The unofficial Beatles Liverpool map that
Colin put together and gave to tourists.

1
Music, Music, Music
(Any time at all)

It was in the late summer of 1962 when I left school at the age of 14 as my birthday fell in late august, at the end of the summer school holidays.

Like most of my classmates at Greenmount Secondary school, in Harpurhey, Manchester, I had trouble getting a job. But, my uncle Bernard put in a good word for me at a back street garage where he used to take his van for a service.

At the Ivy Garage, in Gill Street, Moston, I started by earning 19 shillings and sixpence (93 pence) for a 46-hour working week, pulling my tripe out as an apprentice car mechanic, and that included Saturday mornings. I did everything else but learn mechanics... brewing up, going out to buy food, scrubbing the toilets out and mending punctures. In the winter time, because there was no proper heating in the old wooden garage which had been used as an ambulance depot during the war, I had to try to light one of those old cast iron stoves. What a pain in the arse that was first thing on an icy cold morning. When cars were driven or pushed into the garage covered in snow, all the snow melted and you had to lie on your back on the floor underneath the car's to work on them. I'd work in the wet using pieces of cardboard to lie on because all the flaming lying-down boards had been run over by customer's cars down the years... Happy days!

Like most people my age, I had a passion for listening to pop music. Barry Whittle was my best friend and we would go for a walk every night during the week and at weekends we would go to the pictures followed by a visit to his front room. There we would sit and listen to pirate Radio Luxembourg on his big old wooden wireless. Back then, Luxembourg was the only station that played all the latest pop records.

My passion for music carried on while I worked in the garage and, if a car came in that had a radio fitted, I would go over to it, wind the car window down and switch the radio on. I got told off time and time again by the gaffer Tommy Atkinson who'd shout across the floor: "Switch that bloody radio off!"

Amazingly, this carried on for another 17 years in nine different garages where I worked and in each and every one of them the radios had to be switched on.

Sadly, one of those garages was forced to shut down and I was made redundant. Another three main dealer garages sacked me for accidentally smashing 11 cars up belonging to customers and setting fire to one while I was welding the floor up inside the vehicle. Oops! I was going through a bad spell in my career as a motor mechanic.

One of the accidents was a bit comical at the time. I sent the vehicle ramp up in the air with the car that I was working on, then after a while the buzzer sounded out for brew time so I left the car in mid-air on the ramp. After my cup of tea I came back to the job which was still on the ramp and because I had finished working on it underneath the car, I pressed the switch for the ramp to come down not realising that Billy my mate, (some mate!) had driven into the garage in a rush to get his brew and he'd parked part of a Ford Corsair that he was going to work on underneath the ramp. So, when I threw the switch for the ramp to come down the ramp got so far down and I heard a crunch and then the ramp stopped and wouldn't go any further. That's when I noticed the back end of the ramp was across the bonnet and wing of this Corsair: Oh my! Well, that car had to have a lot of work done to it and I didn't fancy the job the manager had to do trying to explain to the owner of the car that was only booked in for a small job that his Corsair needed a new bonnet and a wing. I'm sure the garage must have started to run at a loss!

When it got to dinner times in the first garage I worked in I would go out shopping for the various food orders the mechanics wanted. I'd set off up and down the main road, buzzing in and out of shops. I hated it. And there was Jack Unal the panel beater who made things worse, always wanting things like a five shilling postal order from the ruddy post office or taking a jacket of he's to the dry cleaners, Any detour like this would mean that when I got back to the garage with the chips, they were stone cold. As a result, all the lads used to go off on one and my name was mud. I would always get buttered muffins and ten Players cigarettes for a lad called Dave Jackson and after all this when the buzzer went we would all sit on the old five gallon oil drums in the corner of the garage having a natter and scoffing the chip muffins from our oily, greasy hands. Bill Sutcliffe would tell us about "the foreigner" he did at the weekend, and Harry Hemmingway would tell us about the bands that he had seen on Saturday night at a coffee bar in Manchester called the Oasis.

When Harry talked about the Oasis I was all ears listening to which groups he'd seen there recently. He'd go on to describe performances by Herman's Hermits, The Big Three, Screaming Lord Sutch and The Undertakers, and loads more.

I thought about how great it would be if me and my mate Barry could get down to the Oasis Coffee Bar ourselves so I called on Barry one night and told him about the place and we agreed to take a trip there as soon as possible. On the following Saturday we caught the bus to town (Manchester) and found the coffee bar in Lloyd Street, just off Albert Square. We stood outside in a little queue and after a while we were inside. Through the door we walked and then down some narrow stairs to the dive bar basement where we paid our 2/6 (12 pence) and wandered into the coffee bar. I immediately noticed the stage. Walking past it and the little dancing area into the place where you could get a coffee or a Coke we had a good look round and as we returned to the dance area we saw the group who were booked to play that night coming down the stairs. I couldn't believe it! Here, in the flesh, were the famous Wayne Fontana and The Mindbenders, bringing all their equipment down the stairs, plugging it in and setting it up on the stage. They would later become the resident group for the Oasis but this was the first of the groups we went on to see over an exciting four year period. A fantastic experience for me and Barry as a week after our Oasis debut we saw Pete McLane and The Clan and gradually all the groups that we'd heard on the wireless and seen on telly. This was our destination, twice a week, and the place to be if you wanted to catch all the top name groups in the sixties and one night while we were waiting to go into the Oasis a van pulled up with the name Herman's Hermit's on the side of it , they were playing that night at the Oasis, they all jumped out of the van and got all their equipment out and set it all up in the street the van driver run a cable down the stairs of the club and plugged it in and before you knew it the Herman's Hermit's were singing to us all, but it wasn't for long because the music was that loud bellowing out across Albert Square the police heard it in the station in the next street and so some officers came round into Lloyd street and told them to pack it in but while it lasted it was a magical summers night of the 60s.

One night, while we were at the Oasis, we went into the next room where they served drinks and where they had the poster on the wall telling everyone who was appearing the next Saturday. In this case it was 8th December 1962 and the poster was advertising a new group playing in Manchester for the first time called The Beatles. We didn't say much because this was just another group that was up and coming from Liverpool where most of the groups came from. At that time in the sixties there was that much music coming out of Liverpool they created a name for called "The Mersey Sound." Even though this new band called The Beatles had been on Granada Reports (which was a TV programme showing all the northern news) and been reported as being a band who were going to make it big, we didn't think much about it because there was so many very good groups knocking about at the time.

The week leading up to The Beatles appearance at the Oasis went by with me back in the garage where I worked and Barry back at the cardboard box making firm in Stockport where he was employed as an engineer, we saved our money as usual and looked forward to going back to The Oasis on Saturday. When Saturday arrived, Barry called for me and we caught the bus again down to town. We got off the bus in Manchester and walked up Fountain Street then round the back of the town hall and into Albert Square. That's when we noticed across the other side of the square a mass of people queuing up outside The Oasis. The queue stretched right up Lloyd Street along Albert Square and down the next street. We knew straight away that there was no chance of us getting into the coffee bar that night. The Oasis probably only held about 500 people, and queuing outside there must have been 1,200…

We just turned tail and went back home. I think we ended up at the pictures. We couldn't understand why so many people had turned out to see this group The Beatles. Every night that we'd visited the coffee bar previously we had always just walked in or, at worst, perhaps waited outside for 15 minutes. And it didn't matter what top group was on, we would always get into the Oasis. Not on this night. Never before had we witnessed anything to compare with the popularity of this new band.

The Beatles' small scale popularity had made a big impression on me and Barry despite the missed opportunity to see them play. But this was just the beginning and no one could have possibly imagined the group's world domination that would follow. We'd seen Billy J. Kramer and The Dakotas, Gerry and The Pacemakers and The Zombies. They were all good but as time went by The Beatles got bigger and better and you couldn't help but notice that they were writing their own music and all their records were getting to No.1 in the hit parade. They were turning them out one after another and they just couldn't go wrong. You didn't even have to buy their records because you could hear them being played constantly on radios everywhere.

When I heard them being interviewed on television, listening to their broad Liverpool accents I realised that they were just four ordinary lads that had grown up in the back streets of Liverpool. Despite their ordinary backgrounds they had great charisma. They didn't talk posh or put on any airs and graces trying to impress anybody.

Britain was leading the way in pop music and I was dead chuffed that groups from the UK were topping the music charts all over the world. The world was at the four Beatles' feet. Like millions of others, I've carried on all my life tuning in to their lives and where they were and what they were doing with their music.

2
Where In Liverpool Did Buddy Play?
(The Empress)

Seventeen years passed and, after moving around Manchester doing the garage circuit as a fully qualified car mechanic, I left the garage trade and got a job working in a factory. Now aged 32, British- Aerospace was where I worked as a pipe-bender in 1979, making all sorts of pipes for all sorts of planes.

I was following in the family footsteps, as all my family had worked at this factory before me. My brother worked in the machine shop in the sixties, during the war my mother was employed as an Itemiser, two of my Aunties riveted panels onto Lancaster bombers and my dad was a turner in the machine shop. My father, Edward Unwin, was well known for volunteering to go on the roof during the war and join the gunner who was positioned there with a machine gun mounted to protect the factory. Dad was the first person to see the German bomber flying in from the south end of the factory on Easter Monday 1941, and he shouted to the gunner "Do something" and had to let off a few rounds of his army issue 303 rifle because the gunner's machine gun had jammed, the two of them must have been scared stiff. The plane dropped three bombs and later my dad told me that he'd seen the roof of the factory open up. The first bomb landed in the machine shop bounced off one of the walls and swiped a row of milling machines across another wall and didn't go off but the second one exploded in the rivet stores and blew hundreds of thousands of rivets all over the factory. The management then got in touch with Henshaws School for the Blind in Stretford and asked if they would give a hand and sort the rivets out and put them in their appropriate bins, just by feel. This saved a good deal of time and prevented pulling a skilled man off the production line to do the job of returning the rivets back into their appropriate metal bins where they had come from. Thankfully, the third bomb landed in the north end yard so nobody was injured.

Decades later, after I'd been working at the factory for many years myself, I became interested in finding out just where the old rivet stores used to be. So I asked one of the older guys if he knew where in the roof the second bomb came in above the old rivet stores. Helpfully, he said: "Come on, I'll show you," and we climbed up and walked along a gantry where he stopped and pointed out the place in the roof where the second bomb had come through and you could still see the difference in the discoloured roof sheeting which had been replaced after the bombing . The full story I gave to the R.A.F. Museum in London and it's now in their records.

I worked at the factory for 22 years and it was hard work because you had to work to a time that was put on the job card and some of the times were impossible to work to. It was bloody hard graft. Your head was down all day long working on the old wooden benches that were issued during the war. I was always glad when dinner time came round and I'd put my feet up on the bench, grab a sandwich and read my mate Tommy Berry's newspaper, which he'd always let me borrow.

I was flipping through the pages one day and I spotted an article about one of my all-time heroes, Buddy Holly. My brother Ted had always bought his records when Buddy started to become famous in the fifties and his liking for Buddy's music rubbed off on me. Even to this day, he is still one of the all-time great singers of our time and a big influence on groups like The Beatles. Anyway, the article in Tommy's newspaper mentioned that Buddy had appeared at a pub in Toxteth in the fifties and I found out that Toxteth was in nearby Liverpool.

So began my active interest in music history and locations. When I'd read the Buddy Holly article in 1992 I had a sudden urge to go and find the pub in question in Toxteth. I bought an A-Z of Liverpool and looked up the name of the street in Toxteth and pinpointed the pub on the corner. I was excited at the prospect of some detective work and I couldn't wait for Saturday to come around. When it finally did, I jumped into my Cortina Mk2 and drove straight to Liverpool. I didn't stop once, and when I turned off the main drag through to Toxteth and followed the map that took me up the side streets, I finally stopped right outside the pub, which was called The Lothian. I was that exited I got out of the car without winding the window up or even locking the bloody car door.

I walked straight into the pub and saw the young landlord talking to his staff. He looked at me as I explained walking in through the door, "I don't want a drink mate. I've read in a newspaper that Buddy Holly had sung in this pub in the fifties and I just had to see the stage as well as the pub." The landlord replied: "We have a stage upstairs mate but it's very small and I don't think it would have been the one and we don't have a stage down stairs." He added: "If Buddy Holly appeared in a pub in this street it would probably have been in the pub at the other end of the street called the Empress." He went on to explain that the Empress was a bigger pub but that he had never heard of Buddy Holly ever appearing there. "Go down and ask at the Empress," he added. "It's just at the other end of the street on the corner."

I came out of the pub and walked down the street, which was called Admiral Grove, and saw the big old pub at the other end. I went in and ordered a half of bitter and then I eventually got round to asking the landlady whether she knew anything about Buddy Holly appearing in this pub in the fifties. Her reply was not what I wanted to hear. She said no but did think Buddy had appeared in Liverpool. She thought that he had played at the Philharmonic Hall and I began to realise that my quest wasn't quite as straight forward as I'd first thought. I felt a bit of an idiot going from one place to another and sat back and sipped my drink in dismay.

Trying to be helpful, the landlady asked me where I was from. When I told her I was from Rochdale she said: "What?

And you've come all this way looking for this pub?" and I said, "Yeah, the things you do!" She then went on: "So you called in on The Lothian at the other end of the Grove and walked down here to the Empress?" When I said yes, she gave me some news I wasn't expecting and explained: "You know you've passed Richard Starkey's old house on the way?" She then went on to confirm that Beatles' drummer Ringo Starr had lived in one of the houses opposite and that the Empress was he's local pub.

I was flabbergasted. Finishing my drink, I asked her for the house number and she pointed me in the direction of 10 Admiral Grove, as I thanked her for telling me where Buddy Holly played and Ringo lived. As I walked out of the pub, down the Grove and stopped outside No.10, I stared at the front door of this old mid-Victorian mid-terraced house and just couldn't believe that one of The Beatles once lived there.

Walking back to my car with Buddy Holly still on my mind, I decided I had to find the Philharmonic Hall I'd been told about. Driving around, I asked a few people, and it wasn't long before I found the place and parked almost right outside the hall. Heading for the big glass doors, I could see that the place was closed but spotted some cleaners inside the foyer Hoovering the carpets. I tapped on the window and one of the cleaners opened the door. Asking whether there was anyone else on the premises, I explained I needed to speak to someone about Buddy Holly appearing there in the hall back in the fifties. Although she said that there was nobody in who could help, she did suggest that there was someone who I might contact. As she was speaking my eyes scanned the foyer walls and I asked whether there might be a photograph hanging up anywhere inside the building of Buddy, but that question also got "no" for an answer.

I couldn't believe what I was hearing. Not to have a photograph on the wall in the foyer of Buddy Holly - one of the three all-time greats in my opinion - who once played there, I thought was disgusting. I quickly realised that I was chasing rainbows trying to find and talk to someone who thought the same as me about Buddy Holly, so I got back to the car and drove home happy that I'd found the place where Buddy had performed but not happy about the place not remembering it with a picture of him on their wall.

Back in the factory the very next Monday, I told Tommy about my visit to Toxteth and finally finding the hall where Buddy Holly appeared. Then I explained how my interest in The Beatles had returned when I'd passed by Ringo's old house twice without knowing and then had it revealed to me by the Empress pub landlady. When Tommy asked me more about how my Beatles fascination had returned and had I been keen on them before, I told him how I'd made a similar journey to Liverpool back in the sixties. This trip was back in 1967 when I worked at Hills Piccadilly garage in Manchester centre. I had a Morris Minor which was my pride and joy and one summer's day in June I took my apprentice for a drive to Liverpool to find where John, Paul, George and Ringo lived. The day out wasn't well planned. I must have been stupid driving to Liverpool and thinking that their houses would jump out at me as I drove round the grubby back streets. We must have driven around for ages wondering if they lived in this street or that street. I must have been day dreaming but I was slammed back into reality when we drove past an old croft at the end of a row of old crumbling terraced houses. There were a gang of scraggy kids playing and when we got up to them one of them picked up half a brick and ran at us before throwing it at the car. I accelerated away from him and was very glad it missed my lovely car. If it had I would have been sorely tempted to catch up with him and make him eat the brick. So, with that, we packed it in looking for where the four Beatles lived and drove back home.

Not put off by my recent visit to Admiral Grove and The Philharmonic Hall, I started getting more and more interested in the lives of The Beatles and where they lived in Liverpool. People at work started bringing in newspaper cuttings and little snippets about them and from one magazine I discovered that Strawberry Field was an actual place and it was just around the corner from where the young John Lennon lived with his aunt Mimi. When I read this I just couldn't get over it.

I started writing addresses down that were printed in those newspaper cuttings and this started a seventeen year itch to journey round Liverpool time after time to find Beatles' places by matching up addresses in an A-Z. Planning properly now, I began finding each location and where it was situated in Liverpool. I couldn't wait to find them.

While working in the factory one day I walked down to the treatments area at the other end of the building and bumped into Howard, an old school mate of mine. As it turned out, he just happened to be as big a Beatles fan as me, so we got on well. I explained to him that I was interested in finding out more about The Beatles and where they lived and I was going to go to Liverpool that Sunday. How said he'd like to join me and I looked forward to what should be a good day out.

When Sunday arrived, I picked How up and we set off. He was that keen, he'd brought along his video camera and started filming the signs on the motorway for Liverpool. We came off the motorway at Knotty Ash and I soon found my way to Queens Drive. This was where Beatles' manager Brian Epstein's family home was in Childwall and when I spotted the number 197 on the door I stopped the car half on the grass verge and gazed at the stone steps that led up to the big five bedroom house. We chatted to each other about how amazing it was just to think about how all the Beatles had walked up those stone steps at one time and Paul McCartney had a cocktail party there for his 21st birthday. We stayed there for a few minutes longer and then drove down the road and turned left, heading for Mather Avenue where Paul McCartney had once lived in one of the streets just off the Avenue.

I overtook a bus that had stopped at a bus stop and I pulled in, got out of the car and ran up to the bus driver to ask him where Forthlin Road was. He raised his arm and pointed to a street just across the road from where I was standing and said: "There it is mate." Beginning to tremble with excitement, I ran back to the car and told How the good news and turned the car round, pulling into a narrow little road. We drove half way down and noticed a little wooden notice board stuck in the leafy garden hedge outside one of the houses. The sign gave the times of the tours to the house which was run by The National Trust, indicating that this was the house (No.20 Forthlin Road) where Paul McCartney once lived.

We were over the moon we had found the place. However, we both noticed that where the gate should have been, there was a chain across the path with a sign saying "Private", so we knew that somebody was living there in the house.

Having parked the car, I started taking photographs and How began videoing the place. I stared at the little terraced house in silence wanting the bricks to leap out at me and tell me the stories of Paul McCartney living on the other side of that brick wall. It just wasn't enough to stand in silence but those bricks wouldn't talk. Never mind, we were still chuffed we'd found the McCartney family home. We stayed another fifteen minutes in Forthlin Road before we set off to find John Lennon's Aunt Mimi's house, named Mendips, where John lived from the age of five. What a day this was turning out to be for How and me.

Mendips was only a mile away but it took me ages to get there because I drove down the wrong back streets to get to it. This kind of thing did happen quite a lot over the years when looking for Beatles' sites and that's probably why I now know certain parts of Liverpool like the back of my hand.

The house was a lovely big semi-detached property where John Lennon once lived with his Aunt Mimi and Uncle George. Driving up on to the kerb, How and me got out of the car and walked up to the front garden gate. I looked down the side and front of the house and at the porch and couldn't take my eyes off it. I'd read that John and Paul used to play their guitars in that very porch because John's Aunt Mimi didn't like the sound of the guitars in the house. Having read the story in so many books, now there was the very place staring me in the face. Then looking down the side garden I caught sight of the little bedroom window over the front porch. That was John's bedroom and had been for 14 years. I had to get a grip of myself and I could have stayed there for another hour standing at the gate just looking at the place but we had another famous place to find nearby.

Strawberry Field, the inspiration for The Beatles' song 'Strawberry Fields Forever', was just around the corner from Mendips on Beaconsfield Road. Reluctantly leaving Mendips, we soon found the right route to a little back road off the main drag into Liverpool. My heart was racing as we reached our destination and spotted the Strawberry Field gates. I drove the car to the right hand side of the road and parked right in front of them. I parked that close to the gates when we got out of the car it was barely three steps and we were at arm's length to the gates - I reached out and put my hands on the cold, cast iron metal work that was bright red in colour. I looked through the gates into the big rambling Victorian garden area where John Lennon played when he was a kid. This was his magical garden and where he got his ideas to write the lyrics to one of his best songs.

While we were standing outside Strawberry Field we were listening to 'Strawberry Fields Forever' playing on the CD in the car. I'd wound down the windows and selected the song to get us in the right mood. The music was echoing through the gardens and all round Strawberry Field itself - so much so that the caretaker came out of the building inside the grounds of Strawberry Field to see where the music was coming from. He glanced at us standing at the gates and then just walked back to where he'd come from.

It did seem odd to me that these gates were known all over the world and yet How and me were the only ones stood there looking at those famous gates in this lonely back street. We read some of the messages on the side stone pillars and on the gates themselves. There were messages written in lipstick, felt tip pen and pencil by fans from all over the world. Some I couldn't read because they were written in various foreign languages. While I was examining the metal work I noticed that on top of the cast iron gates were strawberries created in cast iron as well as the leaf and the flower of the strawberry which were all over the gates. On the top of each of the two big stone pillars were larger strawberries carved into the stone.

Having completed our visit to Strawberry Field we were done for the day and set off for home at the end of an amazing day. The trip had really fired my enthusiasm and I made it a point to buy every book I could about The Beatles' lives and where they grew up. I began pin pointing where these places where on a map, jotting down schools and churches they attended, coffee bars and pubs they drank in, parks they played in as kids and the flat that they shared with an art student friend, Stuart Sutcliffe, who later became a Beatle.

I had to find all these places. So I would visit Liverpool nearly every other weekend over the years with my A- Z and note pad helping me locate addresses which I had jotted down where these four lads once lived.

The more I read the more my passion grew to find out even more and by now I'd read dozens and dozens of books telling me where I wanted to explore. So when I journeyed to Liverpool, turning off the motorway at knotty Ash and driving down Queens Drive, I knew that when I reached the traffic lights at the bottom of the road I was right in the thick of it. Penny Lane was just up the road to the right, the road to the left led you to Strawberry Field and Mendips, Pauls house was only a mile from Mendips and Eleanor Rigby's grave was in Woolton village and the place where she had once lived was close by.

Whenever I drove up to 20 Forthlin Road, I would drop into Penny Lane fire station and have a natter to the lads. Nearly every time I dropped in to the station there was a different watch on so I had to explain (more than once) that I was a big Beatles fan and explain to them the significance of Penny Lane Fire Station. The building actually sat at the traffic lights on Mather Avenue and not on Penny Lane. Also neither the bank nor the barber shop is on Penny Lane as indicated in the famous Beatles song. The confusion behind Paul McCartney's song lyrics may have come about because the teenage Paul would regularly catch the bus going to town and even going to his school and his bus journey would take him past the fire station, the barbers and the bank which were just on the other side of Penny Lane roundabout. The barbershop is still showing photographs in the window and the bank building is still open at the roundabout even though it's now a veterinary clinic.

3
What happened In Allerton Cemetery?
(The missing cross)

One day at work, I read an article in the paper about John Lennon's step sister. Apparently she came over from I think it was America where she lived and made a visit to see her mother Julia's grave in Allerton Cemetery where she was surprised to find the grave with no headstone to it. A bare wooden cross and a stone cat at the side of the cross was all there was to mark the spot and she felt that her mother should have a proper headstone. The newspaper photograph showed her kneeling down on the grass at the side of the cross and it set me thinking.

Allerton Cemetery, it became obvious, was a place How and me had to visit in order to pay our respects to the mother of John Lennon. About three weeks later we travelled up to Liverpool and I drove up to the cemetery where Julia was buried. I knew where to find Allerton Cemetery after travelling around Liverpool for a year or two, so I headed straight for it. As we drove along Menlove Avenue, where Mendips is, I stopped the car just before we got to the house as we wanted to see the bus stop where Julia was heading for when she was knocked down and killed on that fateful night of the 15th July 1958. She had just visited her sister Mimi at Mendips and was crossing over the duel carriageway and tram lines in the centre of the carriageway to get to the bus stop on her way home when the car hit her: Such a sad, sad, end to anybody's life.

We then drove two blocks down the road to Mendips and stopped for a few minutes before continuing our journey to Allerton Cemetery which was about three miles from the scene of Julia Lennon's tragic death. Driving down the main road to the cemetery it dawned on me just how big the cemetery was. In fact, it was so big we didn't know where to start searching for Julia's grave and it was throwing it down with rain. After asking more than half a dozen people who worked there and crossing over different roads to get to different areas of the cemetery we eventually found the right spot. We couldn't see the wood for the trees, as they say. How and I must have walked past the grave seven times before we realised we were in the correct place. It was How who eventually found it first. "Here it is!" he yelled across to me, through the driving rain.

The search for Julia's grave had taken us two hours and we ended up soaked to the skin but we both stood there in silence for a short while, paying our respects and thinking how the whole family must have been devastated when they found out about the accident. I realised that she couldn't have her name put on the cross because anything connected to John Lennon, or any of the Beatles for that matter, especially if it was a material thing, was considered a prime possession to some people. So, to save the torment of the cross going missing the family would have left her name off the bare cross for that reason.

This was the first of many visits I would make down the years to Julia Lennon's (and Stuart Sutcliffe's) graves. One particular trip to Allerton Cemetery in August 2009 I'll never forget. As usual, I parked the car and walked up to Julia's grave and for the first time in nine years the cross was missing. I looked all around the cemetery to see if it was anywhere else but it was nowhere to be found. So I walked back to my car and drove to the front lodge at the main gate. A man responded to my knocking at the lodge door and I asked him if he knew of any reason why a cross on somebody's grave would be removed. He imagined the removal was probably down to the gardener who, when cutting the grass with his mowing machine, must have removed the cross which was in the way. I explained that I thought it odd that he should decide to remove it now, when for nine years I'd been coming here and it had never been removed before. The grass had always been cut around the cross and I'd been round the cemetery and there were hundreds of wooden crosses still stuck in the ground and just Julia Lennon's was missing. The man just shrugged his shoulders. I didn't know just what to believe or what to think, so I got back in my car. One thing was certain. Something needed to be done about the missing cross and I decided that when I returned to work on the following Monday I would make another wooden cross the same size to replace the one that had gone missing.

My place of work was Rochdale Fire Station at the time. I'd been employed there since 2002. That Monday, I rescued some wood and got to work on the cross and made a good job of it, staining it and screwing aluminium stakes to the bottom of the cross so it could be stuck straight into the ground firmly. My wooden replica looked just like the one that had gone missing.

The next Sunday, the 28th August, I drove up to Liverpool and straight to the cemetery. Through the main gates, Julia's resting place was about half a mile into the cemetery. I parked the car and got the cross out of the boot and walked over to her grave where I couldn't help shaking my head to see the lonely space without a headstone and the thought that someone could have taken it. Positioning the cross in the right spot, I then pushed it into the ground and the metal stakes went in firmly and easily. Standing back from the grave, my overriding feeling was that this was a job well done.

A few years later, in October 2012 to be more precise, I stayed with my wife for one night in the Hard Day's Night Hotel at the top of Mathew Street in Liverpool. When I parked my car up and walked back to the hotel I bumped into John Lennon's step sister Julia Baird, who was out walking near the shopping centre. She and I had a bit of a chat and I mentioned the story about her mother's grave. I was very relieved when she was able to tell me that she had the original cross that had gone missing. I was so pleased to hear that.

4
Eleanor Whitefield

(The name on a headstone)

I read in one of my books about the place where John Lennon first met Paul McCartney. St. Peters Church Hall in Woolton Village was the famous location and just across the road from the hall in the church graveyard is where Eleanor Rigby is buried, the lonely woman in the sad Beatles song. When I discovered that the church wasn't very far from John's aunt Mimi's house, How and I went to find the place where the two young lads (John and Paul) met for the first time and started to form The Beatles.

Woolton Village was easy to find. When I got to Liverpool I drove past Mendips and did a left turn round the back of Eleanor Rigby's cottage and into Woolton Village passing the old public swimming baths on the right hand side of the road. This was john Lennon's favourite swimming baths. John loved swimming and joined the swimming club there. As I was driving past, I could just imagine him getting off his bike and walking into the swimming baths with his cossie and towel under his arm. Driving further into the little village, How spotted a church spire over the tops of the terraced houses and we made our way to just what we were looking for - St. Peters. Parking round the side of the cemetery by a little school at the back of the church, How and me walked in through the back entrance of the cemetery and began the search we had decided to make for Eleanor Rigby's grave. We started zigzagging across the rows and rows of headstones looking at every single one finding the name Rigby a few times. Rigby was obviously quite a common name. After looking for about 45 minutes we heard a man's voice ring out across the cemetery: "Who you looking for?"

When I replied that we were searching for Eleanor Rigby he responded immediately: "I thought you were - it's down here mate, I'll show you." Walking us over towards the front of the church he stopped, pointing to the third row of graves. He went on to explain that he was the church warden and he was always being asked where Eleanor's grave was and showed us another name mentioned in the lyrics of 'Eleanor Rigby'. Just two rows in front of Eleanor's was a grave named McKenzie: Father McKenzie being another character in the song. Were these two names on the headstones a distant childhood memory belonging to the song's writer? Nobody really knows for sure except for Lennon & McCartney.

These two people were just names on headstones and nothing more in the lives of John and Paul. Later I discovered that Eleanor Rigby had been born with the name Eleanor Whitefield before marrying Thomas Woods who worked on the railway as a foreman. When he died, Eleanor's grandfather (on her mother's side) asked if she (then Eleanor Woods) would change her name to Rigby as the family name was dying out. So, she died with the name Eleanor Rigby engraved on her headstone. Years later I found Eleanor's half-sister's grave on the other side of St. Peters Cemetery bearing the names Edith and Hannah Heatley.

We couldn't leave the cemetery without a short walk to a dividing fence at the back of the church which separated the church from the school playing field. This was the place where the young Paul McCartney cycled to from his house in Forthlin Road to see a local group called the Quarrymen whose lead singer was a lad called John Lennon. On July 6th 1957 the Quarrymen played for the crowd which had gathered on what was a gala day, celebrating a special anniversary of the city of Liverpool.

I have photographs of John and the Quarrymen performing in that school playing field at the church fete on what turned out to be such an important day. So, when I looked across the playing field to the bank of trees I could just imagine John standing there in that very spot playing his guitar singing his heart out with his combed-back greasy hair, his check shirt and his tight jeans and making his own words up to the song he was singing because he didn't know the correct lyrics.

How and me started to walk back to the church when we caught sight of the church warden again and asked him could he tell us where the church hall was. Thankfully he said yes and explained that he was on his way to make is daily inspection of the hall as he did every morning and we were welcome to join him and take a look inside. How and I looked at each other in amazement. We couldn't believe our luck.

Following the warden across the road and round a small building which led us to the hall, he then pointed to an old wooden door which led to the kitchen and explained that it was this kitchen where Paul was first introduced to John. This was where the Lennon and McCartney association began. The warden then went on to tell us that the door to the kitchen had never been replaced and that the door handles in front of us would have been the actual original door handles that both John and Paul would have used to enter the kitchen on that historic day back in 1957. I took my hand out of my pocket. I had to get a grip of that old brass handle and squeezed my fingers around it before How did the same.

I was disappointed some years later to discover that it wasn't in the kitchen where John and Paul were first introduced to each other for the first time by Ivan Vaughan of the Quarrymen. The real first encounter at the hall turned out to have happened on some old wooden steps that led up to the side of the stage.

After telling his story about the kitchen door handles the warden took us to the front of the hall and unlocked one of the doors and invited us inside. We walked up the dark hall and right in front was a huge stage at the end of the building with what looked like very heavy dusty curtains that were pulled together hiding the windows on the back wall of the stage. At the side of the stage were those famous dusty wooden steps where the 16-year-old John was sitting when Paul (who was only 15) walked into the hall with his guitar in his hand and was introduced to John.

Even now, whenever I go to Liverpool, my first stop is St. Peters Church Hall because this is where it all began for The Beatles. However, on a visit I made in 2002 I discovered that things had changed. The hall had been given a face lift. It was refurbished right through and as I entered the place this time there were plasterers and decorators working inside the hall.

One of the workmen came outside to throw some rubbish in one of the skips and having spotted me wandering around the outside of the hall taking photographs he yelled out: "What you after mate?" I explained that it was just a place I have to visit when I come to Liverpool and that it was where John met Paul for the first time. He looked at me and replied: "John who?" Even when I answered: "John Lennon" I could see that he wasn't that interested but he did say to come on inside and grab a cup as the workmen were about to have a brew. As I made my way inside the hall I noticed straight away that there was a big open space at the bottom of the hall. The stage which had once played such an important part in Beatles history had been taken out.

"What have you done with the stage?" I asked. One of the painters replied that it was all part of the hall's refurbishment and that the stage might be sold off to pay for some of the work that needed doing on the old building. When I asked where it is now he told me it was down in the cellar. I was mortified and the plasterers could see it in my face. Supping my tea, I went on to explain how I felt that it should have stayed in the hall. I tried to explain why, the decorators just sat there supping there tea, listening to me ranting on.

There was nothing I could do. The decision had been made and the stage had been removed. The heart of the hall had been ripped out and all I could do was sit there with the lads drinking my tea and every so often turn my head and look at the big empty space where the dusty old stage once stood.

The workmen asked me where I was from and when I told them I'd come from Rochdale they couldn't believe I'd come all the way to Woolton early in the morning. But I told them that I had to come, again and again, because this place meant so much to me.

Where we sat having our brew was the dance floor and there were heaps of the old wooden parker tiles scattered all over the floor that once formed the actual dance floor itself, The workmen had taken them up and were using them to patch up parts of the floor that had been taken up near where the stage had once stood.

Paul, one of the painters, got up off his chair and walked over to where some of the loose tiles lay. He shouted out: "Col!" When I looked up one of the tiles was in mid-air heading straight for me! As I caught it, Paul shouted: "Here's another one... keep 'em." Paul had given me two tiles. I was blown away, thinking how John and Paul could have walked on the tiles 45 years earlier and now they were mine. The Woolton Church Hall tiles are now in a frame which hangs on the wall in my Beatle room at home.

The next time that I travelled to Liverpool was a fortnight later and the decorators were still working in the hall at Woolton. I just walked in and they all let on to me. Luckily I'd arrived at brew time and the workman called George headed over to put the kettle on. When one of the others said they would be going out to get some toast I said I'd volunteer to do that if he'd tell me where the café was. Given directions to the village I took the order and walked down to the café and put my order in for 12 rounds of thick toast with plenty of butter. "You must be hungry," said the girl behind the counter as she laughed to which I replied: "Yeah. I'm starving!" as I handed over my £5.

When I got back all the lads said thanks for the toast to which I told them they were welcome. It was a hot summer day so we had our brew outside, plonking chairs in between the skips and scaffolding. While enjoying our tea and toast they began telling me about the Magical Mystery Tour bus that came to Woolton about three or four times every day and how funny it was especially watching the tourists on the previous Friday. That day there had been a group from Japan. As usual the tourists were dropped off at the entrance to the little car park in front of the hall and they walked up to the building. As soon as the group caught sight of the skips full of rubbish that had been taken out of the hall they headed over to the skips and clambered up the sides. One of the Japanese tourists nearly fell right into one of the skips as he began to collect pieces of plaster and another had found a bent rusty nail to keep. They just wanted some sort of Beatles memento and obviously anything would do. All of the plasterers and painters came to the door of the hall to watch them scavenging and fell about laughing. They couldn't believe what they were seeing and that someone could treasure a piece of plaster or a rusty bent nail. John the painter asked me if I would treasure something in the same way and although I replied that I wouldn't I did have my eye on something that I did think had some special Beatles interest. Pointing across the car park, I indicated a spot in front of the building on the floor of the car park. There was an outline of some walls that once formed an outside toilet. We were at the place where John Lennon first met Paul McCartney and where they later played on the famous stage. The two must surely have used the toilet back all those years ago! Although the toilet had been pulled down, left behind were the porcelain trough and a little cast-iron grid at the end of it. All the Japanese tourists had walked across the car park and passed right by what was left of the toilet, never realising that John and Paul probably peed in that trough many times! When John the builder responded by mentioning that the land all around the hall was going to be tarmacked over, filling in and covering the trough forever, he added that I might as well take the grid if I wanted it. Then, to my delight, he got up, walked over to his van and reached for a six-foot crow bar out of the back and returned to the grid and began striking the pointed end of the crow bar into the middle of the grid. He barely had to put his weight behind it and just let the weight of the crow bar do its work. He dropped the crow bar to the floor and the little grid popped out stuck on the end of it. Pulling the grid off the end, he then threw it to me. "Cheers," I said as I caught it with one hand. I thought the rest of the lads would be laughing but none of them were. I'd been coming to that hall for five years and never thought that I'd own the grid that John and Paul peed in!

When I got home I soaked the grid in bleach and then scrubbed it with a wire brush before framing it. I couldn't put it on the wall because Lynn and the kids thought that I was potty, to coin a phrase.

I often think about the lads that were working on the hall and what they must have thought about me taking home an old toilet grid. I slowly got to know some of their names and when they introduced themselves one was called John, one was called George and two of the others called themselves Paul and Ringo! Although they were taking the Michael, I just had to laugh because they were such a great bunch of lads.

The roundabout at the end of Penny Lane.

The Woolworths shop that John used to wait outside, for Cinthia Powell to finish work on the cosmetic counter.

John Lennon's favourite swimming baths in Woolton Village.

The original stage before it was taken out of
St. Peters Church hall in 2002.

St. Peter's Church Hall in the background, where John Lennon was introduced to Paul McCartney in 1957. In the foreground is what was left of the outside toilet.

Eleanor Rigby's headstone which lies in St. Peters Church grave yard, and whose name could allegedly been used in the famous song.

5
Walk That Walk To John And Paul's
(Don't pass me by)

Over years finding the locations where the four Beatles grew up, I realised there was a special route that both the young John and Paul took to get to each other's houses. So, in July 2002, I decided to make the trip to discover where they walked. One of the books I had gave the names of the streets that they had used but on finding out that they passed through the park at the side of Allerton Golf Course the trail went cold. My reference book didn't give directions to just where the path was located and I assumed the author didn't know himself. I needed to do some detective work.

Determined to find this unknown path and not pass it by. I made a weekend trip to Liverpool, parking the car on Wheatcroft Road which led up to the gates of Allerton Golf Course. This was the road that Paul and John used to and from the park when they went visiting one and other.

I walked into the park looking for any path that I could see and quickly spotted some golfers in the distance. Approaching them I asked if they knew if the path we then stood on led to Menlove Avenue (where John Lennon's home was). Explaining that it did, they directed me to keep on walking for 15 minutes before it reached Menlove Avenue. I carried on and about 15 minutes later I did reach Menlove Avenue but could see that this entrance to the park was too far up the road from John's aunt Mimi's house to be the one that John and Paul used. I knew there must be a nearer entrance that they both used and began walking back into the park and spotted a second group of golfers some distance away. Heading towards them I zig- zagged across the open golf course keeping an eye out for flying golf balls.

Apologizing for interrupting their game I enquired whether any of them knew of another path that might lead through to Menlove Avenue. One chap said that they didn't know but that "Bob would" and pointed to a man wearing a yellow jumper getting ready to tee off on the next green. Thanking them, off I walked again and when I got to Bob I asked him the same thing. Pointing out the path I'd already unsuccessfully tried, I asked him if there was another to Menlove Avenue. "Yes," he said. "There's another one and it runs past an old cottage in the park itself." Pointing me in the right direction I set off again and after ten minutes I came across the cottage and a path next to a sign saying "Private No Way Through." This stopped me in my tracks. I was getting pretty fed-up chasing rainbows again and began to doubt whether I'd ever find the path, so I called it a day.

By the time I'd returned to the car I wasn't put off because in a week I'd try again. Then it would be a bit easier, as I knew two of the paths that I had tried were the wrong ones and surely the next one I'd discover would be the right one.

I drove to Liverpool the week after and decided this time to park my car in the side street opposite the McCartney's family home in Forthlin Road and walk from there. When I walked up to the top of the road I saw John Halliday standing there. John was the custodian who lived in the McCartney's home and I recognized him straight away having seen him on the television. He was waiting at the top of Forthlin Road for The Beatles tour bus to arrive, a point from where he'd walk the tourists down the street to the McCartney's home and show them round what is a National Trust property. He met the tourists in this way because the National Trust like to keep the neighbours happy and didn't want their small tour bus driving down this little road all day long annoying the neighbours. While John was stood there waiting for the bus I stopped and asked him if he knew where the path was through the park that john Lennon and Paul McCartney used. Happily, he said that he knew it very well and used it himself when walking to Aunt Mimi's house. Mendips was also a National Trust property and John would keep an eye on it and even sometimes let his son Paul stay there and act as security for the house because there was no one living there full time. Pulling a piece of paper and a pen out of his jacket pocket, John sketched a map of just where the path was located from the main park gates. I was dead chuffed with this little map and thanked him. Just then the bus pulled up and John went over to meet it introducing himself as the custodian as the doors opened. As the tourists stepped off the bus for their tour I walked away to finally try and find the long lost path.

Before following John Halliday's map I returned to the car to get my big old fashioned video camera out of the boot and a tape recorder I had brought with me. My plan was to make a video that I could watch at home on television anytime I wanted to walk that walk. I began videoing while walking down the main road which was a duel -carriageway, and after a while I noticed that all the cars on the main road were slowing down as they approached me. Some cars were flashing those coming in the other direction. They obviously thought that it was a speed trap! Imagining I was getting their vehicle numbers, no doubt that was why I received a couple of V signs from the drivers.

As I walked I videoed Wheatcroft Road, the road that led up to the park gate and I wondered if any of the people living in those houses were living there 45 years before catching the odd glimpse of two lads walking past their front doors with guitars over their shoulders. What a picture that conjured up. At the top of Wheatcroft Road I crossed over the street at the top and reached the entrance to the park where the golf course was. Here I got the map out and followed John's sketch sticking to the left hand side of the park where a line of trees stood while remembering that when John and Paul walked past these trees they must have been just little sprigs. Arriving at the last tree I could see the start of an almost hidden path that veered off to the left. There was the old park wall on one side of it and on the other was the fence surrounding the golf course. I switched my tape on playing old Beatles songs because there had to be a background of their music being played while I was videoing and walking along.

I was in my element, knowing that 45 years earlier John and Paul had walked these very steps with their guitars slung over their shoulders, probably singing the song that they had written that very day. After about ten minutes I noticed all the golfers that were playing in the field at the side of me seemed to be looking at me while I was walking along the side of their golf course. It suddenly dawned on me why. They were, all trying to get on with niece quiet game of golf while here was me forcing them to listen to Beatles music that was thundering out across the golf course. I just carried on walking and playing the music and getting black looks, thinking it's only the once, not realising at the time that I had to walk back the same way later playing the same loud music.

I enjoyed every step that I took along the narrow dusty path, my walk only disturbed by a man taking his dog for a walk to whom I said hello. On reaching some cottages, with lovely gardens which were on the left hand side of the path, I could hear the sound of traffic. Noticing a path dropping down and leading on to the pavement of Menlove Avenue with some old stone steps, I went down these and stood on the last step and looked down the road. I could see Aunt Mimi's house in the distance and continued videoing and playing the music as I headed towards Mendips. More strange looks from passing motorists again - it was another duel-carriageway, with me and my big old fashioned video camera walking along the pavement looking for all the world like a motorist's speed trap. Nothing could bother me now. I was nearly there at my destination: John Lennon's childhood home.

On reaching the opposite side of the road to Mendips I started to cross the duel carriageway. What a headache trying to talk into the microphone at the side of the video camera while watching the oncoming traffic from both directions as well as trying to carry on videoing the place in front of me where I was headed. Glad to reach the other side of the road, I walked up to the gates of Mendips and stopped for a few minutes. Then I turned around and started to walk back the same way still videoing the route right along Menlove Avenue, I was getting used to those signs I was getting off the drivers by now when I got up to the stone steps I carried on through the park again. I bet the golfers couldn't' believe their ears when they heard the Beatles music bellowing out across the field again. When I finally reached the McCartney's house I switched the music off and spoke into the microphone before switching that off too. Just as I'd finished, the door of 20 Forthlin Road opened.

6
The Door Opened To 20 Forthlin Road
(Step inside)

John Halliday had seen me dozens of times over the years, as he gazed out of the window of Paul McCartney's childhood home. He'd also seen me outside Mendips, taking photos. So, when he saw me on the day I videoed John and Paul's walk route he came out of 20 Forthlin Road and walked up to the front garden path to chat. "You're a real fan aren't you?" he said and continued. "I saw you last week and here you are again and even though you're a big Beatles fan you never walk up to the front door and ask to see inside, why?" "Well", I replied. "It's the house where you live and you have a sign across the garden path that says "Private" and I respect that and I would never knock on your door." He went on to say that he'd seen me walking past so many times, or just stood outside taking photos, and asked me if I was planning to return to Liverpool next week. When I replied that I would, along with my friend How, he responded by inviting us to come inside 20 Forthlin Road and have a cup of tea before showing both of us round the McCartney home.

    I just couldn't believe what I was hearing. It never entered my head that John Halliday would invite us in. Accepting his invitation I said: "Thank you very much, you don't know just what this means to me and How."

    I couldn't wait to get back home to tell How. When John asked where I lived and I replied "Rochdale" he said I must be a real fan to come over to Liverpool almost every week.

Back in Rochdale I couldn't wait till Monday to tell How the good news so I phoned him up and told him that next Sunday we were invited to be shown round 20 Forthlin Road by the custodian John Halliday. How nearly fell through the floor. I told him that we had to be there early before the first tour started and How readily agreed that whatever time I decided to pick him up he'd be ready.

The week seemed to drag along in the factory and when I told some of my mates I had an invitation into one of The Beatles' homes I got mixed reactions. Older blokes were chuffed for me and How and the younger ones had nothing to say, probably because they didn't rate the Beatles. Lynn and the kids couldn't believe it when I told them that How and me were going to be shown around the McCartney's home.

When the morning of Sunday 19th July finally arrived, I picked up How and we headed straight for the McCartney's home in Allerton, travelling at what seemed to be six feet off the ground up the M62. Our heads were buzzing with excitement.

We felt like the bees knees when we arrived outside Paul's house and walked up to the chain across the garden path, with the sign saying "Private" and began actually unhooking the chain to walk down the path to the front door. A knock on the door saw John answer the door with Molly his dog, who was jumping up all around us. We made friends with Molly straight away.

Having introduced How to John, we were ushered in, walking into the house's small living room where we were invited to sit down on an old sixties-style couch which took us right back to the days of The Beatles. Everything in the house was fifties and sixties style to make the house look just like it did when Paul lived there. While John was in the kitchen brewing up, me and How sat there taking everything in. There was a piano, old-style wallpaper, an old standard lamp that stood in the corner, a tiled fireplace and many interesting photographs hung on the walls.

John came in and spotted me standing up staring at the photographs on the wall and explained that all the pictures were taken by Paul's brother Michael (Mike) McCartney when he started to become an up and coming photographer back in the sixties. He went on to mention that the two photographs near the door were of John Lennon and Paul when they were practising with their guitars in the very room we were in. Cleverly, the pictures were hung in the rooms where the photographs were actually taken, which made the house come alive, capturing a time before these two musical minds were known to the rest of the world. The photographs on the other side of the room above the piano pictured Paul on his own, sat on the piano was one of his Dad Jim and another was of his brother Michael on a drum kit. I couldn't take my eyes off the photographs, viewing them on the spot where they were actually taken.

John said that any chance that Michael got he would snap a photo at any time of Paul and John and even Dad Jim. He went on to say that all the photos had been lent to the National Trust by Michael who owns the copyright and that none of the public visitors to the house were allowed to take photographs of them. The prohibiting of photography was just one of John's tasks at Forthlin Road, another was the restriction of visiting hours. John described the constant knocking at the front door day and night. It just didn't seem to matter what time it was for some Beatles fans to try and get to see inside the house. Some fans even demanded entrance to the house and to be shown around because they were members of the National Trust. He would always have to explain that the only way to get in and look around is by booking a trip on the tour bus that takes you to John Lennon's aunt Mimi's house first and then Paul McCartney's home, both on the same trip. There was no other way because 20 Forthlin Road was also the house where John Halliday lived as well as worked as the custodian of Paul McCartney's childhood home.

John had plenty of stories about the house and told How and me about the night he was woken up by the revving of a car engine right outside the house with bright lights shining up to the bedroom windows. Pulling back the curtains he saw two very bright headlights from a car that had mounted the pavement to get a direct shot of the house with the lights on main beam. Dressing quickly, he had gone down stairs and opened the front door to find two Americans standing on the pavement at the front gate videoing the house!

When John asked the pair what they were doing at such a late hour they explained that they had hired a car during the day and drove it all the way up from London finally arriving at Forthlin Road in the dead of night. They'd driven the car onto the pavement because it was dark and they wanted the front of the house lit up to film it and record a commentary that night because their plane was leaving in the morning to fly them back home. This was their last and one and only chance to video Paul McCartney's house. Although they tried their hardest to do so, they failed to smooth talk John who responded in that cool Liverpool manner: "Just do one, or I'll phone the police!" With that, they got back in the car, had about three bites to get back off the pavement and then drove back up the street to the main road and John went back in the house and straight to bed.

After John had told us this story he said to How and me that if we'd finished drinking our tea he'd show us round the house. Taking the empty cups from us he beckoned us to follow him through double doors into the dining room. There on the wall in front of us, next to the window, was a photograph of Paul and his Dad Jim in the back garden reading the same newspaper. Paul was reading it over his Dad's shoulder and his dad was sat on a deck chair. According to John, Paul's Dad was stuck on a crossword and when Paul had asked him which question he was stuck on, Jim replied: "Mailbag." Paul asked: "How many letters?" and Jim replied "hundreds of them!" Michael McCartney had taken that photograph from the dining room window, the reason why the photograph was hung on the wall next to the window.

Next, John guided us into the kitchen with its tiled floor and old original kitchen sink the McCartney's used. The tiled floor was original too and when John showed tourists round the house he would always tell them that this floor in the kitchen had been stood on by all The Beatles, manager Brian Epstein and Pete Best so they could kiss the floor if they liked! Some did, usually North American ladies who would get down on all fours and perform the kissing of the floor. John went on to say that there weren't many original fittings in the house that were there during the McCartney's time. Nevertheless, there was still a good collection of authentic items. There was an old fashioned washing machine and cooker and on the wall was an old wooden shelf that had cups and saucers on it as well as plates - just how it was when the McCartney's lived there. And to prove it there was a photograph of John Lennon in the dining room of him stood in the kitchen waiting for the kettle to boil and next to him was the old wooden shelf on the wall. There was another photo of Jim looking shocked washing his son's socks in a bucket in the sink. At the time the picture had been taken Michael had shouted to him and when Jim turned around Michael snapped him with is camera.

John told us that the National Trust got the house back to just what it looked like when the McCartney's lived there by asking Michael to take them right through the house and tell them what wallpaper, light fittings and furniture had been in every room. Next on our guided tour we left the kitchen, passed down the hallway to the bottom of the stairs and headed for Paul's bedroom. On our way up I asked John if the banister rail was the original and he said yes, so I gripped it till I reached the top of the stairs remembering who had gripped it all those years before. John led the way into the small bedroom on the left hand side of the landing and when we joined him inside he told us that this was Paul's bedroom, the smallest bedroom even though he was the oldest son. Apparently, when first moving into Forthlin Road, he did have the biggest bedroom but later on when Michael started to become more interested in photography they swapped over rooms so that Michael could develop his skills with that hobby.

The contents of Paul's bedroom amazed us. Apart from his bed, all he had was a small bedside cabinet and one chair with two photographs on one of the walls. One pictured Paul apparently sat on a chair with his leg drooped over the arm of the chair looking cool but actually he was hiding a big rip in the arm of the chair so that the photograph could be taken. After How and me had given the room a good coat of looking at we walked onto the landing and John pointed out his own private bedroom where he slept. He told us that the bedroom used to be Dad Jim's and Mum Mary's room. This and the bathroom were the only two rooms in the house that were kept locked and not accessible to the public as there was a modern shower in the bathroom that didn't fall in with the late fifties / early sixties decor when the McCartney's lived there.

As we walked into Michael McCartney's back bedroom, I noticed a photograph on the wall next to the window of Paul climbing up the drainpipe to the bedroom window. All the history I had read about t Paul's house suddenly all came together and one story in particular. I'd read years ago that when Jim was out at work the empty house was the most convenient place for John Lennon and Paul to practice their music. However, Paul didn't have a house key so he would go round to the back of the house and climb up the drain pipe to the toilet window and squeeze himself through the narrow toilet window. This window was always left open so Paul could slide in headfirst but he always dreaded that his brother Michael or his Dad might have left the toilet seat up resulting in a nosedive straight into the pot. Having entered successfully through the window he would run down the stairs and let John and his guitar in through the front door.

When I had finished looking out of the bedroom window at the drainpipe I noticed another photograph on the back wall and asked John who the two people in the photograph were. It turned out they were Paul's uncle Albert and his Aunt Millie who were pictured both flat out asleep on the couch in the living room. The reason that they were so tired was because when Paul's Mother Mary died of breast cancer his Uncle Albert and Aunt Millie regularly travelled across the water from the Wirral where they lived to Forthlin Road to do the McCartney's washing and ironing. It was during one of these visits that they both flopped down on the couch and fell asleep and Michael snapped them with his camera.

Years later Paul wrote a song called 'Uncle Albert/Admiral Halsey' when he went solo and Michael recorded the song 'Lily the Pink' when he used to be in a band called The Scaffold in which Auntie Millie gets a mention. Paul's 'Uncle Albert/ Admiral Halsey' was an American chart-topper and 'Lily the Pink' was a No.1 in Britain.

When How and me had finished having a look in Michael's bedroom, John walked us down stairs into the living room and asked if we wanted another brew. Happily accepting we finished the cuppa and said our goodbyes. We couldn't thank John enough for showing us round and could have stayed there all day but had other Beatles places in Liverpool to visit. He said we were always welcome and gave us his telephone number so we could just give him a ring next time we were coming. When How and me got back into the car we couldn't get over what John had said.

Next on our list was the Jackoranda Coffee Bar situated near the famous Cavern Club, a place where John, Paul, George and Stuart Sutcliffe would go to for coffee and toast.

To find the Jackoranda I parked the car in the Albert Dock car park and then headed across to Mathew Street. How and me searched high and low walking up and down side streets to find the place and finally spotted it. Entering the Jackoranda, we ordered a cup of coffee and sat down.

I'd read that down in the cellar of the Jakoranda there were murals on the walls painted by John, Paul and Stuart. When short of money to buy coffee and toast the three lads were asked by the owner, Allen Williams, if they would paint pictures all over the walls in the cellar as he knew that they were art students from the local college. The association with Allen Williams didn't end there. He would later become the first manager of The Silver Beatles.

Leaving my coffee I tried to open the cellar door but discovered that it was locked. So, I asked the barman if I could go down and have a look around for the murals. The barman said "no" as the place only opened on Thursday nights. I was a bit sick about this but in the end How and me drank up and left without seeing those paintings on the wall.

When I got home and went into work, (which was now Rochdale Fire Station because I'd got a job there as the janitor after taking redundancy at the factory), the lads at the fire station asked me if I'd done anything at the weekend. When I told them that me and my mate had been invited into Paul McCartney's house in Liverpool they were dead chuffed for me. They knew that I was a big fan of Paul and The Beatles because I had photographs of them on the walls where my locker was.

From then on whenever I visited Liverpool I would call in at 20 Forthlin Road. But, always before arriving, I would go for my breakfast at Tescos (not Tiffanys!) and then buy some meat pies and scotch eggs for John Halliday and myself for dinner. By this time I'd got into the routine of helping John out every time that I went. He'd asked me if I would help him by asking the tourists for their cameras as they weren't allowed to take any photographs in the house. So, I would ask for their cameras and belongings and lock them away safe until they were leaving, then give them back to them when they were ready to go. John also asked me to mingle with the tourists and answer any questions that they asked because he said that I knew as much as he did about The Beatles, in fact probably even more.

Helping out at Forthlin Road seemed to be going very well and I did it many times over the years. When dinner time came round we would take Molly for a walk and, on our return, sit down and relax   listening to some old Beatles' songs that I brought with me on my tape recorder. Singing along to all the records seemed surreal sat in Paul McCartney's house. Some were songs he'd never sang in his own house and just visualising him in the very room I was in, practising with John Lennon, I couldn't possibly get any closer to my idol. My mind went back 40 years to the day I couldn't get to see The Beatles in my local coffee bar in Manchester.

The ban on photography proved difficult to police. Confiscating cameras on the way in didn't stop all photography. In later years I would mingle with the tourists to check they didn't use cameras that were on their mobile phones. John would ask them to have their mobile phones switched off and out of sight. My being there did improve security in other ways too, because I would be upstairs while john was downstairs talking to the tourists.

On one occasion we said goodbye to a group of tourists and waved them off at the front gate then set off taking Molly for a walk round the local streets. John and I were about to learn some new Beatles' history. The walk was one we usually did at dinner time after the tourists had gone and we walked passed a row of houses in the next street. On reaching the last one we heard a voice shout out: "Hey do you live in Paul McCartney's old house?" We both stopped and John replied: "I do. Why?" Coming up to the fence, the man said: "Well, I've seen you on the television a few times. I thought that I recognised you." He went on to explain that he had been told by the old owner who lived in the house before him, when he was buying the property, that the garage at the side of his house that belongs to the house is the actual garage that Paul McCartney once rented. Apparently, when Paul lived in Forthlin Road, he escaped to the garage to get away from the girls that would wait for him in the front garden at No. 20, on his return home every night.

Renting the garage in the next street to Forthlin Road meant that he would drive there instead and lock up his car, then head for home by shimmying down the side of the garage to a hedge. Climbing over the hedge he'd then cross the large field, used as a police training ground, in the grounds of their collage and make for his own back garden fence before scaling that to enter his back garden, then he would walk in through the back door into his the house, through the kitchen . Meanwhile all the girls were waiting for him at the front of the house and he would then see them all through his front living room window.

A few years later in 1964, the McCartney's moved to a house in Heswall on the Wirral to enjoy a bit of peace and quiet. They moved at night, so there was less chance of any girls taking mementos out of their boxes of belongings that were being shifted from the house into the removal van.

After listening to the story about Paul's garage, which John had never heard before, we got back to No.20 Forthlin Road after finishing taking Molly for her walk. We had to prepare for the next three house tours. As custodian of the house John's tour began by meeting the group at the top of the street and walking them back down to the house. His skill in the role shone through every time he began speaking to the tourist groups in the living room. After his own introduction, John would introduce me and explain: "All cameras and belongings that Colin has taken off you will be returned after I've given you a call telling you that there are only five minutes left for you to have a last look at anywhere in the house." He'd then instruct them saying: "The front door will be open for you to go outside and take photographs in the front garden, if you like."

After talking to them in the living room, John would show them around the house telling them stories about the McCartney family moving into the house in 1955 and how Mother Mary died a year later, leaving Father Jim to bring the two boys up on the very low wage that he got. John would show them into each room and tell the tourists about each and every photograph that was hanging on the walls, introducing a story for each of them. The tourists were always mesmerized by what John had to tell them. His memory for dates and events, when asked questions, was always amazing but he also had the knack of entertaining visitors with his special sense of Liverpool humour. Many of the visitors to Forthlin Road from around the world would write to him when they returned home after their trip. Beatles' fans from as far away as Japan, Canada and Australia would request photos of John, standing in the doorway at No.20, as a memory of their tour and the man who became something of an international celebrity as a result of TV appearances around the world in his role as custodian to the McCartney family home.

7
For The Benefit Of Who?
(Rochdale not Bishopsgate)

When visiting Liverpool I always called into any Beatles shop to have a look round at their collectables. The first shop that I found was in Albert Dock, mainly because I used to park my car there and walk through to get to the Cavern in Mathew Street. The shop was run by two young ladies and we always had a good laugh when I went in. I remember on one occasion buying some Beatles' postcards, one of which was the Victorian poster of Pablo Fanque's Circus. I found it interesting because John Lennon bought the original poster from an antique shop in Sevenoaks Kent when The Beatles were in that area making a promotional film for 'Strawberry Fields Forever'. The words on the Victorian poster turned out to make up most of the lyrics to the song 'For the Benefit of Mr Kite', which was one of the tracks on their Sgt. Pepper's Lonely Hearts Club Band album. John used all the names of the circus characters and their acts in the lyrics. Mr Kite was William Kite, son of a circus proprietor James Kite. He was an all-round performer in 1810 and is believed to have worked in Pablo Fanque's circus from 1843 to 1845.

When I got home with the postcards I studied the one that advertised the Victorian circus, printing all the acts that were appearing in the circus. In big bold letters it read: "Being for the BENEFIT OF MR KITE" and at the top of the poster it printed the name of the place where the circus show was held.

It wasn't as the Sgt. Pepper lyrics read: "Mr Kite performs his feat on Saturday at Bishopsgate." Instead, imagine my surprise and delight when I read the words at the top of the poster that said "Town Meadows, Rochdale." As I was living and working in Rochdale it became more interesting for me to search for where Town Meadows was. When I asked the lads at the fire station they said that Town Meadows was just across the road from Rochdale Town Hall, right near the police station. So, when I had time, I walked down and crossed over the main road from the Town Hall and spotted the street sign "Town Meadows" on a low stone wall, which was part of a small bridge that crossed the River Roch in the middle of Rochdale.

I wanted to take some photographs of the spot, so the following Sunday I got some bunting together to add a circus theme to the photograph and took the flags down to Town Meadows. I rigged the bunting up onto the top of the bridge wall and then took some photographs, hoping all the time that the police didn't come out of the police station that was right at the side of where I was and move me on or book me for parking on double yellow lines.

A few days later the local paper got hold of the story and printed it. As a result my research found its way onto the internet and on the 15th February 2007 I received a letter from a Mr Max Kite living in Salisbury, Wiltshire. He wrote to tell me that he was trying to track down his family tree and had traced his Great, Great, Great Grandfather Charles Kite, who had married and lived in a place near Rochdale called Todmorden. He'd done some research on the internet to find out more and my name had come up and the fact that I lived in Rochdale and seemed to know a little bit about the place where the circus had been held. His letter filled me with enthusiasm to go and find out anything I could about Mr Kite in Todmorden.

The very next Sunday I drove to Todmorden and parked up at the back of St. Marys Church where Charles Kite (Max Kite's Great, Great, Great Grandfather) had married Elizabeth Moyle. I began searching row after row of headstones to see if I could find the name Kite. A look at every headstone didn't reveal a single Kite name. As I started walking back to the main gate of the cemetery I saw a man walking up by the church gate and I approached him to ask whether he knew of another church in Todmorden. "Yes," he replied: "There is another old church which is not very far from here called Christ Church." He helpfully pointed out where to go and find the church. I jumped in my car and drove up to this old croft which was across the road from an ancient looking disused church. I got out of my car and started my second search looking round what was a huge cemetery for any headstone bearing the name "Kite". Doing my best to find anything, I had to push my way through thick bracken and some heavy weeds and even balance on old walls that were crumbling with age. Many of the headstones were covered in mould which had to be wiped away before I could read any inscription.

After spending hours searching, I realised when I started to get to the end of the last row that this was not where Mr Kite was buried. I was so disappointed but all I could do now was walk back to my car, clean my hands with an old rag that was in my car boot and drive back home. When I got home I sent a letter to Mr Kite in Salisbury to tell him what I had done and that there was no trace of Mr Kite being buried in Todmorden. He wrote back and told me how grateful he was for the time and trouble I'd taken in looking for the headstone. That appeared to be the end of the trail but there was still further information that was to come my way about Rochdale's Beatles connection.

Later that same year Rochdale Library started a project called 'Rochdale Rock' all about singers and songwriters through the years that were somehow connected to Rochdale. So, I called in to the library workshop called Touchstones and told them about the story of John Lennon and the Victorian poster advertising the circus in Town Meadows. As it turned out, they had read about my story in the Rochdale Observer a while back and they were glad to hear that I wanted to give them all the information I could so they might add it to Rochdale Rock.

After a week or two the people that were doing the work for Rochdale Rock told me that when they went down into their vaults to find out what they had in their archives about Pablo Fanque's Circus Royal appearing in Rochdale they found an old poster. It was advertising that same circus but it was dated a few months later and was advertising for the benefit of somebody else, not Mr Kite, this time. So, if the antique dealer that owned the shop in Kent had purchased this poster dated a few months later than the one John Lennon bought, John's song could have had a different title entirely. Possibly something like 'For the Benefit of Mr Sidebottom' … who knows?

8
A Lady, A Dog And Two Chinese Girls In The McCartney's Back Yard

(What a tale to tell)

Helping John Halliday over a period of years and coming into contact with so many people from different parts of the world, there were always incidents and stories to tell about the interesting Beatles' fans we encountered.

Before each new tourist group visited 20 Forthlin Road, we always got a phone call from the coach driver telling us that he was on his way and how many were on the bus. On one occasion in June 2004 the driver told us that there were four Americans that had booked to go on the tour that hadn't made it to the bus on time. So, they had hired a taxi to take them to the house and they might be a little late.

As John put the phone down from taking the call from the driver he turned to me and told me what had happened. Then he instructed me that if they arrived late, and he was in the middle of talking to the tourists in the living room, I wasn't to let them in if they knocked on the door. Thinking, I'll just wait and see what happens and that they might still be on time, we both waited until the bus arrived. Ten minutes went by and then the bus pulled up and John showed the group into the house. I did a head count and discovered that there were four people missing. Taking the group's belongings as I usually did, John then began talking to them in the living room as I stood in the hallway. After five minutes there was a loud banging on the front door and John stopped talking to the tourists, turned to me and said: "Don't let them in." He then carried on talking to the tourists and the person at the front door just carried on banging. When John had completely finished his introductory talk he walked over to me in the hall, unlocked the door and let the four latecomers in.

Straight away he asked them to prove that they were the four Americans that missed the bus. As this was going on, a rather big American woman from the four walked up the hallway to me and flung her arms around my neck. She screamed out in a very loud, broad American voice: "This is where Paul McCartney lived. He lived in this house." Then she just burst out crying, sobbing her heart out while the others were still producing their permit badges for the tour. This American lady just wasn't coming up for air. We just couldn't console her. So, in the end, we got a chair for her and asked if she would like to sit outside in the garden and get some fresh air. When she agreed, we unlocked the kitchen door and let her sit there and this in turn made it a little quieter. Now at least the tourists could hear John speak to them over the racket that she was making which lasted until it was time for her and the rest of the tourists to go. She had travelled all that way and not even seen the McCartney's house all she had seen was the McCartney's garden. John went into the back garden to tell her that the bus was waiting outside and presented her with a flower that he picked from the garden. She had stopped sobbing at this point and was delighted with the flower. John asked her if she was alright as he escorted her to the front door and all she could say was that she was sorry. We both saw her safely onto the bus and then waved her goodbye. What started off going pear shaped on that tour thankfully straightened itself out in the end.

There was another incident at Forthlin Road I remember well around this time. John and I had just seen the first tour off onto the bus and John had said he would take Molly out for a walk asking me to stay in the house and I said: "Okay. I'll get the brew on for when you get back."

They'd only been gone ten minutes when there was a knock at the front door. I looked through the curtains and saw John and Molly. As I opened the door John said straight away: "Get hold of Molly. There's been an accident at the top of the street on the main Road and a dog has been knocked down by a car."

He then went running off to the top of the street and I took Molly in and shut the door. Five minutes later John was knocking at the door again and when I opened it he stood on the doorstep with a big black dog in his arms. He beckoned me to open the back door and he followed behind me carrying the dog which he lay down in the back garden. I went and got a bowl of water for the dog which was obviously suffering. Severely shocked, the dog's tongue was hanging out and it was walking round the back garden in circles barking at thin air.

Thinking what to do next, John said: "There's another three tours this afternoon and we can't unlock the kitchen door for the tourists to have a walk in the back garden because they will see the dog and wonder what's going on." I agreed and we sat there waiting for the second tour.

It didn't seem long before the bus arrived. John went out to meet them and acted as though everything was fine showing them round the house while the injured stray dog was in the back garden walking around and barking at nothing.

All three tours went well and when the very last tour group were ready to be picked up by the bus driver and they were outside in the front garden taking photographs a taxi pulled up. This was a common occurrence. All day long, seven days a week, there were private cars and taxis pulling up at the front of the house to have a look where Paul McCartney once lived. John knew all the taxi drivers and this taxi driver came over to John and me and said that he had noticed an accident that morning at the top of the main road when he was driving past. He'd heard that John had picked a dog up off the road to look after it. John told the driver that the dog was in the back garden walking about still suffering from shock. The taxi driver said immediately: "I will have it. I'll pick it up later on." I couldn't believe my ears, I was so glad to hear that he obviously loved animals and felt sorry for it and was willing to take charge of it, even though it was a stray and had no name tag or collar.

Later, that afternoon, I was relieved to hear a knock at the front door and there was the taxi driver who had come to pick up the dog. Both John and I let him into the back garden and by this time the dog had settled down a bit. The taxi driver picked it up and walked through the house and out to his taxi gently putting the dog on the back seat of his cab. We said: "Cheers mate" and he drove off.

This was just another example of John's calm handling of a difficult situation that came right out of the blue. He'd just carried on in his cool custodian manner, talking to the tourists while a traumatized dog barked its head off and a hysterical American Paul McCartney fan sobbed her heart out in the garden. Hats off to John!

Another testing tour day at Forthlin Road occurred one sunny morning when an unusually small group arrived at the house. While the number of people on the tour bus varied from time to time, most times there were thirteen visitors on each trip.

When the bus turned up that day, there were just two sweet Chinese girls on board. John, who knew a few words in different languages, said hello in Chinese and the two girls were tickled pink. Both girls could only speak a few words in English or understand it, so John had to mainly use all the photographs around the house to do the talking.

They had come a long way to see the lovely city of Liverpool and visit Mendips and Forthlin Road. When they were shown into Paul McCartney's house both girls had their hands clasped together and their heads slightly bowed forward as if in prayer. As they walked in, they were both very quiet as they were shown every room in the house. They smiled all the time and occasionally nodded their heads while John was trying his best to let them both know all about the McCartney's living at Forthlin Road.

Even though nothing was said, both girls seemed to be enjoying their visit. When it was time for them to go, John said goodbye in their own language and they both replied. We both walked them to the front gate and John reached over to the garden hedge, pulling a few leaves off the bushes as he did so. He gave them to the girls and they clasped their hands together trapping the leaves in the palm of their hands. Then one of the girls opened up a magazine that she was carrying with her and placed her leaves in between the pages and then closed it before saying "thank you" - one of the few phrases that she could say in English. We waved them off and when we walked back down the garden path I joked to John that you could pull leaves off the hedge, bottle them and then sell them to tourists. We both laughed and went back into the house.

9
Walking Through Calderstone Park
(Like dreamers do)

I phoned John Halliday one day telling him that I was in Liverpool the next day and I knew that it was a day that he didn't work. He said: "Yes come over. We'll have breakfast in the café in Calderstone Park and I'll point out some places that you'll be interested in."

John Lennon's Aunt Mimi's house (Mendips) is on one side of Calderstone Park and Paul McCartney's old home is on the other side. When I got to Forthlin Road that Sunday, I told John to bring Molly so she could have a run out. We all clambered into the car and shot off to the park. As I pulled into the car park, John told me that this was the car park where all the media and television cameras were camped out in 2000, waiting for Paul McCartney to arrive in his car when he was due to unveil a plaque. The plaque was to be dedicated to his wife Linda and positioned in the children's playground that Paul had sponsored in her name.

At the moment Paul was due to turn up the media waited in the car park but he caught them unawares by coming into the park from another entrance and walking in behind them! All the cameras were facing the wrong way. When asked about how he knew another entrance to the park he explained that this had been his favourite park as a kid and he knew (and remembered well) all the entrances into it. Explanations over, Paul walked over to the play area and unveiled the plaque.

When John, me and Molly started walking through the beautiful park, John turned to me and said: "We'll walk this way around the lake and I'll show you the spot where I met Paul and Jane Asher in 1967." John had mentioned this before, as I recalled. He'd come across Paul and his girlfriend Jane when working as a gardener in the park that year.

As we skirted the lake, the path opened out and met another one that was on a slight incline. Here, John stopped and pointed to an area full of flower beds. He remembered that he and his mate were digging out the borders ready for the flower beds when his mate looked up and spotted Paul McCartney with a girl walking a dog. His mate shouted over to John: "Look there's one of The Beatles!"

As a keen fan of The Beatles, John straight away stopped his digging, stuck his spade in the soil and walked over towards Paul. He realised that the person Paul was with was Jane Asher and that the dog that they were taking for a walk was in fact Paul's dog Martha, famous as the dog who appeared in Paul's song, 'Martha My Dear.'

When John reached Paul and Jane they stopped and he managed a long chat. Paul had all the time in the world for John and he told him about a new Beatles record that they were ready to release that following week. As they were talking, John and Paul were both stroking Martha's coat and their hands on the back of Martha met – a magical moment I thought. So well did the two get on that they carried on chatting until eventually John had to explain that he would need to get back to his flower bed. John left Paul and Jane saying what a pleasure it had been to meet them and returned to his mate to inform him that The Beatles were releasing a new record next week! When John next looked up from his work he saw Paul and Jane in the distance on the other side of the lake and couldn't quite believe who he had just met and talked to.

Some years later, when we took Molly for a walk in the park, I asked John if I could take a photograph of him and Molly on the very same spot where he'd met Paul, Jane and Martha on the path all those years ago. Knowing the story behind it, the photograph I took is a picture I will always treasure.

Paul McCartney may have loved the park but it also held a few memories for John Lennon too, being just across the road from his Aunt Mimi's house. As a favourite place of his, I was determined to find the secret places he visited and follow up the stories I'd read about John Lennon and Calderstone Park.

Joined by all his mates from school, John and friends would ride their bikes through the park .They would all cycle up to an area of high ground just up from the lake, a place they called "the bank". On reaching the top, they would get off their bikes and sit on the grass while John searched in his pocket for his harmonica. When John placed the instrument to his lips and began playing, all his mates would start singing the latest pop songs of the day that they had heard on the wireless.

With a good view of the park, this spot of high ground was perfect for a sing song. John and his mates could spot anybody that was walking and getting near to them. The minute they did see anybody getting close, they would stop singing and John would put his harmonica back in his pocket.

On one of my many visits to Liverpool I drove into the park and then wandered up to the lake. It didn't take me long. I knew exactly where the lake was and when I'd reached it I walked round to the other side where I saw the field start to climb upwards slightly to a few trees that were at the top.

There's a bench half way up the hill, so when I got up to it I sat there for a while looking at the clump of trees to the back of me thinking that this was near enough the place where John and his mates from school, (who later became the Quarrymen) would sit and sing their hearts out. I had a feeling of peace and sadness about this secret place of John's because it was one of the places where he enjoyed going to when he was a young boy. It probably seems so insignificant to a lot of people but the feeling that I got when I went there was that hardly anybody knew about it or was interested anyway. For me to find this lonely spot that John loved going to, which few people were aware of, seemed sad. As I sat there thoughts of his life, cut short and assassinated by a nobody, filled my head.

After I'd sat for a while on the grass bank contemplating these thoughts I stood up and tried to find the route that the schoolmates took from this secret place to another nearby location and a story about John that somebody told me.

The story is about a place in the park very near to the grassy bank and I Imagined John and his mates, disturbed from their singing, making their way out of the park, heading in the direction of the Calderstone Road entrance.

Cycling along this path they had to ride past the famous Allerton Oak Tree to get to the gates at Calderstone Road. The famous Allerton Oak is a 1,000-year-old tree to the side of the path. When they reached it a few of them rode on but John stopped his bike, got off, then walked over to this ancient tree. Reaching up into the branches he pulled off a single leaf and turned to his mates, who had stopped to watch him. Here he made his now famous prediction. "One day I'll be one of the most famous people in the world," he said, then got back on his bike and cycled off with his mates to the gates of the park.

To find the Allerton Oak, I made my way from the high ground along the path to the Calderstone Road park entrance. I must have been walking for about five minutes when I caught sight of a huge tree just at the path's edge. On a small cast-iron fence around the tree was a plaque describing the age of it and what used to go on hundreds of years ago when people would use the spot as a meeting place.

I stood there for quite a while looking at the tree. Then, realising that me standing there in a lonely part of the park staring at a tree might look a bit odd, I decided that the next time someone passed by on the path I'd tell them the John Lennon story. Two young women then passed by walking a dog and I said: "Good morning." As soon as the dog heard my voice it came over to me wagging its tail and began jumping up. I continued talking to the dog but it was just hysterical although the owners just carried on walking until they were dots in the distance. They kept on shouting at the dog but it wouldn't leave me and in the end one of them had to walk all the way back to me and pick the dog up. "It's took to you," said the woman and I replied that I was about to make off with it. She laughed and asked me not to talk to the dog again until they were out of sight as we said our goodbyes. Clutching the dog to her tightly, she carried it off into the distance. I had my last look at the old tree and then I was on my way.

At the side of the huge cast-iron main park gates on the corner at Harthill Road are four big stone figures called the Four Seasons. These stone figures all stand on a low wall and it was on the wall that John Lennon would stand entertaining and telling jokes to his classmates in the morning before the school register was called. A group of his mates would congregate here before every school day, as the place was conveniently close to where they were headed at Quarry Bank Grammar School, just down the street. These 'audiences' were perhaps the beginning of John becoming used to facing and entertaining a crowd, even if they were only his school mates.

Colin and Howard started out together to find out where in the back streets of Liverpool, these four lads grew up.

Roseberry Street, where the quarrymen played on a flat backed truck.

John Lennon's second favourite park where he went for a walk to console himself just after his mother was knocked down and killed.

Litherland Town Hall Ballroom, before it was turned changed into a walk in clinic.

The grave of Stuart Sutcliffe with the headstone leaning forward.

Ringo lived on Admiral Grove, which stands to the right hand side of the Empress Public House.

The Four Seasons gates entrance to Calderstone Park.

10
A Day To Remember In Mendips
(And it wasn't the last)

On a day I'd arranged to go to Liverpool and take How, I phoned John Halliday and he told me that the National Trust was in charge of Aunt Mimi's house Mendips after it had been bought by John's wife Yoko Ono, who in turn had given the keys to the trust.

So, in addition to the National Trust property at Forthlin Road, John told me that he now had the keys to Mendips as well. He went on to explain that he was in charge of the security of the house before the National Trust got all the builders in to take the house back to looking like it would have done when John Lennon lived there. John Halliday had his son, Paul, living there because someone had to always be in the place that could never be left empty. He finished the phone call by saying that he'd show both How and me round the house when we arrived.

How and me couldn't get to Liverpool fast enough! When we pulled up outside the McCartney's house, we went in as John was just washing out Molly's food dish. When he'd finished that he said: "Come on, we'll go now".

We all got into my car and Molly jumped on to John's knee as we set off and it seemed to take barely ten seconds to get to Mendips. I stopped on the grass verge in front of the house, something that I'd always been used to doing when I'd been there before over the years but this time John jumped out of the car and said: "I'll open the gates. Just drive in". Saying "drive in" sounded so special and made this day, 28th of July 2002, one that I'll never forget.

We got out of the car and walked up to John, who was unlocking the front door of the porch before he unlocked the inner door that led into the hallway. Invited in by John, I stepped into the porch and stopped and looked at the very place where John and Paul used to sit opposite each other playing their guitars because John's Aunt Mimi would banish them from inside the house. We then walked into the hallway and then followed John into the living room as John said he'd get a brew on. John was always obliging with the brews. I looked around the room as we waited. Were these the chairs that John sat on and was that the fireplace where he would warm his hands in winter? John Halliday then came in with the teas and started telling us about Mendips and that nearly every piece of furniture in the house belonged to the person who lived in the house after Mimi had moved out.

Getting up off the settee I walked over to the big bay window and looked out across the front garden that was now overgrown. I had looked at these windows from the outside for years and never thought that one day I would be on the inside looking out.

When we finished our tea John said he'd show us round the house, starting with the dining room and the kitchen, then the back room. We then followed John up the stairs and I remember running my hand along the banister rail and counting the steps on the stairs. Turning right at the top of the stairs, we then walked into John Lennon's bedroom. Although it was only small, the bedroom was dwarfed by a big wardrobe on the left hand side and on the right was John's bed. It wasn't John's original bed but to me it looked old enough and to me it was John's bed where he slept. Near the window was a little old dressing table and looking back I noticed an old air vent that was in the actual brick work. The vent was high up on the wall at the side of the bed. I just knew that it was there when John lived in the house. How many times had he stared up at that air vent just before he nodded off to sleep?

Having shown us the bathroom, John led us down the stairs and as I got near to the bottom step I noticed that the ceiling was low and wondered how many times John Lennon had ducked his head thinking that he was going to hit it.

We then walked through the dining room and kitchen into the back garden. Heading for the garden hedge at the back, I looked for the part of the hedge where John would have pushed his way through for a short cut to get into Strawberry Field and the big rambling gardens where he played as a kid. His Strawberry Field 'playground' was the grounds of a Victorian children's orphanage run by the Salvation Army. I often wondered if John used to play with the kids from the orphanage. If he had, he must have asked the kids why they were all living in the one big house. What would he have made of their replies when they told him they were all living there together because their parents couldn't look after them?

After me and How had looked round the back garden and the house we all walked down the hallway and out the front door. John then locked the door because his son wasn't in the house but on his way to Mendips to look after the place from his girlfriend's place. Driving back to Forthlin Road I dropped off John and Molly and we thanked John for showing us Mendips. Big hearted as ever, he said again that we were big Beatles' fans and we were his friends and were welcome anytime.

Before returning home we drove down to the Cavern Club. We'd been there many times before. Not the original Cavern Club, it was moved to the other side of Mathew Street, then pulled down and then moved back to the original side of the street but in a different place, (two shops further down the street from where it was before). Even knowing all this past history of the place, when you walked down those stone steps into the cellar and heard music being played, this was still The Cavern. The only thing that was missing from the days when the walls ran with condensation as The Beatles played their lunchtime sessions for the local secretaries and shop and office workers was the smell of bleach that they used to wash the walls down with. When we'd had enough in there we walked down to The Grapes, a special pub in Mathew Street where some of the groups appearing at The Cavern would go for a proper alcoholic drink. Sadly, it was the pub where Pete Best infamously called for a drink when he was told by Brian Epstein that The Beatles wanted Ringo Star as their drummer and not him. Pete walked round the corner from Epstein's N.E.M'S record shop into Mathew Street and called in The Grapes for a drink.

Another time I called on John Halliday on one of his days off. He invited me to join him for a drink on a visit to a new bar that had opened on Penny Lane. We enjoyed a beer together and John asked if I minded a trip to the nearby Woolworths across the road. He was looking for a book to read and I said no problem. We supped up and walked over to Woolworths and on the way John told me that this was the shop were Cynthia Powell worked for a time on the counter. She had moved across from the Wirrel to get nearer to the art school she was attending and nearer to her boyfriend John Lennon. So, while John Halliday was busy combing the shelves for a book, I asked one of the ladies that worked there if she knew anything about Cynthia Powell (John Lennon's first wife) when she worked at Woolworths in the late fifties / early sixties. She listened to my request then shouted to a workmate who was across the shop. Her mate came over immediately and she said to her: "We've got a Beatles' fan here." We all three of us started laughing and she said I thought that she'd heard me talking about Cynthia Powell working at the shop. She confirmed: "Yes, Cynthia did work here in the sixties" and pointed to the cosmetics serving counter. "That was the counter she worked at" and went on to explain: "Every Friday Cynthia would ask the boss could she go early and the boss always looked towards the two big double-fronted windows because each time the same dark figure of a man stood there with his back to the window." This was of course John Lennon waiting for Cynthia to finish work, so that he could take her to the pictures or somewhere else he'd planned for their date.

Years later the Woolworths shop shut down, but I still stop and tell the story when I pass the building, doing my day tripper tour around Liverpool with friends. I also point out, just across the road from there, the little church (St. Barnabas) which is actually at Penny Lane roundabout. This is the church where Paul McCartney sang in the choir and years later (in 1982) where his brother Michael got married. Keeping as low a profile as possible, Paul was the best man and it was quiet when they turned up at the church. By the end of the service, they came outside to find the pavements packed full of fans trying to get a glimpse of the McCartney brothers.

I've walked down Penny Lane many times and on one occasion I did it videoing while walking to the other side of the roundabout and up to the barber's shop, which must be half a mile away, playing Beatles' music all the way. No wonder people gave me a wide birth, they must have thought that I was potty, wearing a black mac borrowed from work trying to recreate the story in the song 'Penny Lane'. When I arrived at the bank on the corner, where the roundabout is, I hung the mac on the door handle of the bank, because, as the lyrics say: "The banker never wears a mac in the pouring rain ....very strange." So I hung the coat there on the bank door handle and videoed it: "Very strange!"

Wandering down Penny Lane I turned down a side road called Dovestones Road to visit the primary school that John Lennon and George Harrison attended as kids. Because of their age differences, neither future Beatle ever met in the school or playground but my research had told me that this was the school where John possibly picked up the few words from a poem that was going around the schools at that time and later used it in 'I Am The Walrus'. Those never-to-be-forgotten words were: "Yellow matted custard, dripping from a dead dog's eye."

After I had taken some photographs of Dovestone Primary school – as it was a Sunday there was no problem taking pictures - I walked back to Penny Lane roundabout. It suddenly struck me that all the places on the 'Penny Lane' song are not actually on Penny Lane: the bank and the barbers shop are not and the fire station is half a mile away on Mather Avenue.

Fortunately, there was no problem with my next location being where it should be. When I took my wife Lynn for her first Beatles trip to Liverpool we called at a terraced street called Arnold Grove. We'd planned a visit to see the house where George Harrison was born on 25th February 1943. The house is in a little back street cul-de sac. Here at No.12, George lived with his two sisters and one brother and of course his mum and dad until 1950 when they all moved to a new council estate in Speke. While we were there, looking at George's old house, we were spotted videoing the house by an elderly lady who lived in the end house of Arnold Grove. She came out of her house and called us over: "I can see that you're interested in George Harrison, because I heard you mention his name when you were talking to your wife," she said. She then proceeded to invite us into her house to tell a little story about George, who she obviously remembered well. Explaining that her son was George Harrison's friend, she told us how they would both play in the street and the way they would always enter her house by running down the lobby straight through the living room and kitchen and into the back yard. "Those were the days when you left your front door wide open in the summer time and the both of them used to rush through like that," she recalled. I thanked her for asking us into her house and telling us her little story.

11
From Behind A Curtain
(I saw you peep)

On many occasions I took friends to see 10 Admiral Grove, where Richard Starkey once lived. There was one visit I remember better than most. This time, as we approached the door I saw a face of an elderly lady peering through the net curtains and then the front door opened.

A nice old lady, who we later discovered was called Margaret, came to the door and asked us if we'd all like to come inside. We all piled into her very small living room where she said that some of us could sit down and the others would have to stand. She said that she had seen me many times before, talking to people outside the house and I explained that it was the first place that had started off my interest in finding out where all four Beatles one lived and grew up.

Having introduced herself, Margaret went on to say that the only reason that she had asked us all in was because my friend's wife was with us and she didn't feel threatened if she let us all in in the company of a woman. Those of us that had found a seat sat down and Margaret brewed some tea for us all. We couldn't help but notice all the photographs on the walls. There were dozens of pictures of Ringo and his family and when Margaret brought the teas in she just stood in the middle of the room (there was nowhere left to sit anyway!) and told us all about Ringo and his mother moving into this house from Madryn Street, which was just across the road at the top of the

Grove. Ringo was five when his Mum and Dad split up and that's when they decided to move to Admiral Grove because the rent was cheaper. Back then, in Ringo's time, the house had been a lot smaller. Since Margaret had been living there as a tenant, the house had been extended with a kitchen and the back yard had been fitted out with a new garden.

Margaret went on to tell us tales about some of the tourists that had turned up at her house from different parts of the world. Sometimes she would let them in but only after she had looked at them through the net curtains first.

She remembered one group of fans in particular. They were a bunch of German tourists that she invited in. According to Margaret, although they were all big men, one of them started to cry when she asked them if they'd like to come inside. Overcome with emotion at being invited into Ringo's old home, Margaret gave the man a cup of tea and, after telling the group stories about Ringo and his mum living there, she asked them to sign the visitor's book. This they all did and got up to leave, telling her how good it was of her to let them into her house.

Having seen them to the door she waved them off, thinking that would be the last she saw of them. A couple of hours later on she got a knock at the front door and when she opened the door she found all the Germans had returned and were stood in a circle right outside her front door. One of the Germans beckoned her to step outside and stand in this circle and when she did, they all started to sing a song to her for being so kind and letting them into her house. And they weren't done yet! When they'd finished their singing, one of them gave her a big bunch of flowers. Slightly overwhelmed by all this, Margaret told us that she thanked them all for the flowers and wished them a safe journey home, waving them off again for the second time.

After Margaret had finished telling me and my friends that story, I said that it was time for us to go. Just as she did with those German fans, she wanted for us to all sign the visitors book, which took a while because there was so many of us. When we had all signed the book, we thanked her for her hospitality.

From that day, whenever I go to Liverpool, I always pop into to see Margaret and have a natter with her over a cup of tea and a biscuit. Just like the Germans, I took her flowers once and she told me that she didn't like flowers so I started taking her biscuits instead. During my visits she tells me all the latest news and what's going on in Liverpool on The Beatles' front. Whenever it was time for me to go I always had to sign my name in the visitor's book, again and again. I've been that many times I'm sure I've filled one of those books on my own.

When I say goodbye to Margaret and walk back to my car, I think of that first day when I was looking for the pub that Buddy Holly played years before and walking passed a house not knowing that Richard Starkey once lived there. It was the day my passion for finding out more about The Beatles began.

I always park my car opposite the Empress pub, at the corner of the street, when I call on Margaret. This was Richard Starkey's local pub and it has been immortalised by Ringo, pictured as it is on the cover of his first solo album, Sentimental Journey, released in 1970. Commemorating this fact, the pub has had this information set in a stone plaque placed over the main front window for all to see when the Magical Mystery Tour bus stops outside on its tour round Liverpool.

Back in my car, after I've been to Margaret's, I always put on a Billy Fury CD. Billy, real name Robert Wycherley, was the first rock star in Liverpool. I play the CD because he and Richard Starkey went to the same primary school, which just happens to be across the street from the Empress pub.

I have driven around Toxteth a few times, searching for 34 Haliburton Street where Robert Wycherley lived. The area was easy enough to find but not the street. There have been many changes since Robert was a boy. Newer houses stand in the place where his childhood home would have been. I'd built up my hopes to find the house where Liverpool's first rock star lived but that was never to be.

When I head back to the city centre from Margaret's, (the same way that I come) I always pass street upon street of Victorian houses and the car seems to know its own way. I'd been to Liverpool that many times visiting the same places it wouldn't drive past Roseberry Street without turning down there. It's a car with a mind of its own at times.

Roseberry Street was well known to have been the street that the Quarrymen played while on the back of a flat back coal lorry in 1957. The lorry turned into the street and pulled up at the kerbside and the group sang to the people that gathered to listen to them. This performance was part of a special event for the city of Liverpool. On the 22nd of June 1957 people were celebrating the 550th anniversary of King John's royal charter to Liverpool. That day, there were parades all around Liverpool with people in costumes on flower filled floats parading through the streets.

After John Lennon and the Quarrymen had set up their equipment to play to the crowds gathering in Roseberry Street they started to sing. At this moment one of the band members noticed a couple of teddy boys getting John Lennon in their sights, intent on causing him some trouble. So, the music stopped and the band grabbed their equipment and took safety at No. 84 Roseberry Street where a Mrs Roberts let them in to her house. Because she knew them and she was one of the organisers of the event, she allowed them to take refuge until a policeman arrived and escorted them all safely to a bus stop to get home.

When I visited Roseberry Street on 15th February 2004, the old terraced houses had been pulled down. All that stands there now is a bare croft, but I can still imagine walking down the old street with the old terraced houses there just as it used to be. This is because many years ago, when I first found Roseberry Street, I videoed it as it was when the coal lorry stopped at the pavement ready for the Quarrymen to play to the people, allowing me to relive the moment on my TV.

12
The Teddy Boys Mean Trouble
(Stuart was in the middle)

Driving across to the big Anglican Cathedral I knew that I was in the area where a part of The Beatles' ever-changing lives evolved. I searched around and found the ground floor flat that Brian Epstein rented at 36 Faulkner Street during 1961 and 1962 for £4 per week. Then I walked across the road to the pub in a narrow side street that John Lennon and Cynthia Powell did a bit of their courting in.

The pub was called "Ye Crack" and as it was the nearest pub to the art college in the next street a lot of students would use it. Calling in for a drink I sat at a table in the back room choosing one that looked like the table that Stuart Sutcliffe had a photograph taken at, which I have in an old book at home. Aside from being a place Cynthia and John visited this was also the pub where Stuart and John used to go to chat about art and music.

Finishing my drink, I then walked to the top of Rice Street where Ye Crack was and crossed over the road heading onto the next block where Stuart and John lived together in a flat at 3 Gambiar Terrace. It was here the two Beatles lived, painted, played their guitars and slept on the floor.

My interest in Stuart Sutcliffe grew greatly after watching the film Backbeat which showed him befriending John Lennon at art collage and meeting Astrid, his girlfriend, in Hamburg. The film covers his short life and his very tragic death and how he became an acclaimed artist just before his death.

After reading about Stuart's life in Liverpool over the years, I found out where his flats were and where he did his painting. The discovery of his flat at 53 Ullet Road I remember well. This flat wasn't far from Blenheim Lakeside Hotel which later became the Sutcliffe's family home. I visited 53 Ullet Road by arriving early one morning on the 11th November 2003. Walking up to the flat I noticed that the front door was open and there were old bags of sand and cement in the front garden along with planks of wood and other building materials. I got out of my car and walked up to the front door and started to video the house. Shortly afterwards a van pulled up at the front of the house and three men jumped out with hard hats on. They walked up to the front door where I was standing and one of them asked: "Are you OK mate?" I said: "Yeah I'm just videoing the house. Is it all right with you?" When asked why, I told him that this was once Stuart Sutcliffe's flat, one of The Beatles, and how I was a big fan. "Stuart Sutcliffe? Don't know him mate - but Frank will," he responded, turning to his mate who was getting some tools out of the van. He then shouted over to Frank: "Do you know who Stuart Sutcliffe is?" and explained what I was doing. Fortunately Frank did know who Stuart Sutcliffe was and shouted back at his mate: "Let him go in if he wants." "Cheers mate," I responded, and straight away walked up the stone steps past the front door and into the hallway.

When I was inside the house I could see that the place had been taken right back to the bare minimum. There were bare walls and dusty floorboards and I ran up the wooden stairs, thinking that if Stuart had chosen any room in the house it would have been the front bedroom overlooking the park across the road.

I walked into that room and just stood there. My eyes were all over the place looking at the bare floorboards for paint colours that could have dropped from Stuarts paint brushes while he was working, but there were none. Walking over to the big window, I looked across to the park wondering if Stuart ever stood there doing the same thing.

When I'd finished talking to myself, I left the bedroom and walked down the stairs and out the front door stopping on the stone steps that lead up to the front door. "Are you off now?" called out one of the workmen. When I replied I was and gave my thanks, he said: "Your right mate."

I walked back, got in my car and drove down the lovely back road around Sefton Park to the Sutcliffe's family home. Now a hotel called Blenheim Lakeside Hotel, it overlooks the lake in Sefton Park. When I headed up the stone steps to the front door I noticed a brass plaque on the right hand side of the door which said that the building was once Stuart Sutcliffe's family home. Reading the plaque, I was surprised that the Sutcliffe family once lived there. The building was immaculate and the views over the park were breath-taking. When I walked into the hotel I was even more surprised to see all the photographs on the walls of Stuart and the early Beatles which were photographed by Stuart's girlfriend, Astrid, in Hamburg.

Inside the hotel, I sat down and had a coffee with Colin the landlord and he pointed out to me two rooms that the Sutcliffe's rented on the bottom floor of what was now the hotel. He went on to say that Astrid had visited the hotel not very long ago. While on the subject of visitors interested in The Beatles, I was surprised to hear Colin say on a future visit of mine that he had received no other interest from visitors since I was last there. He was disappointed the place just wasn't drawing the public's interest. Perhaps very few people came because the hotel was off the beaten track. Maybe if it had been smack bang in the middle of the city it would have been more attractive to the tourists especially around the time of the release of the Backbeat film.

Another story I was keen to follow up involved Stuart. I'd read a few books that said there had been a physical attack on The Beatles at the ballroom at Litherland Town Hall. Confusingly, some books said that the incident had taken place at Lathom Hall, which was just about a mile down the road from Litherland Town Hall.

I had to go and see these places for myself. Over the years I made many visits to Litherland Town Hall but the first time I ventured there was with How. On that day we approached David, the hall's security man and asked him if he knew anything about the ballroom dance's that they had there in the late fifties and early sixties. Helpfully David told us that he used to be a part of the management team in the sixties and was involved in all aspects of running the ballroom dances at Litherland Town Hall. He said he was always glad to see anybody with as much interest in The Beatles as How and I had and he asked us to wait for about ten minutes until it was time for him to do his rounds, checking everywhere was secure. When the time came he reappeared and said: "Follow me". We then walked down corridors to some stairs and when we reached the bottom David unlocked a door before entering a hallway and another door. On opening this door we finally entered a huge ballroom with a big commanding stage all set up with curtains pulled back to the side, as if ready for some group to appear and do their gig.

We were all ears listening to what David said. He pointed out holes at the edge of the dance floor near the walls and explained that these were the fixing holes for seats that were screwed down around the dance hall, which have long since gone.

Then David said: "Come on, I'll show you the changing room where The Beatles waited to come on stage." Following him round the back of the stage along a dingy passage, he stopped at a door on his left hand side and invited us in to the changing room. How and I walked in to what was a very small room which led into an even smaller one with a sink in it. Glad that I had my video camera with me, I got everything on film. Even though the changing room had no seats or table, just some litter on the floor and a sweeping brush leant against the wall, this was the place where John, Paul, George, Ringo, Pete Best and Stuart Sutcliffe got ready to go on stage. This was my heaven!

Coming out of the changing room I asked David if I could stand on the stage and he said: "Of course." So I walked up these dusty old wooden stairs at the side and then walked into the centre of the stage, looking out across the full length of the hall. I stood there in silence remembering that The Beatles stood there when they had just returned from Hamburg to play their first main venue.

David went on to show both of us the old wooden ticket kiosk near the main entrance to the ballroom. He even went outside and unlocked the steel shutter so we could see just how it looked when The Beatles played the place. How and me couldn't thank him enough.

Because David knew so much about the hall, I asked him if he'd heard anything about the teddy boys that The Beatles were supposed to have met up and fought with at Litherland. According to some reports in books I had, a fight had taken place in the car park outside the hall on January 1961, although some reports suggested that the fight was at Lathom Hall just down the road. David said that he'd never heard of the fight being there at the hall but said if it was anywhere out of the two venues it would have been at Lathom Hall. "There was trouble nearly every night there," he said. "It was the toughest area around here at the time for fighting with teddy boys. They controlled the area and they wouldn't take no shit from anybody. There were fights at the drop of a hat - it was rife."

I told David that I'd go round to Lathom Hall another time. So, before we set off for home, How and me thanked David once more for showing us the hall and for telling us some of the things that he knew about the place. We said our goodbyes and I told him that he'd be seeing me again. Here was another important place in Beatles" history that I'd never forget.

I had actually already been to Lathom Hall some years before but now I knew more about its history from David and through my Beatles books I made another special visit. On the day I chose to go it was throwing it down with rain but that didn't put me off. Arriving at Lathom Hall I turned off the main road and down the side street that led up to the building and then stopped at the front gates to the car park. As I got out and started filming the front of the place two cleaners were stood at the front door of the hall having a fag. They watched me for a while and then shouted to Brian the landlord. When he came to the front door the girls pointed me out and all three were looking at me, wondering what on earth I was up to.

Brian shouted to me to come over and asked why I was so interested in videoing the hall. When I told him that The Beatles had played there and that I wanted to get it on film he invited me in. "Come on inside mate and have a look round," he said. helpfully. I was over the moon because I would get to see the stage where The Beatles played. When we walked in through the door I was amazed to see a number of life-size figures of Elvis Presley, Marilyn Monroe, and I think John Wayne was there. In addition there were advertisements for Coca Cola and burgers all over the place. I said: "It looks a lot like an all American bar – you've done a lot of work in here," and he said: "Yes - and I haven't finished yet." Then I asked him where the stage was and he told me that it had been removed many years ago. My mouth dropped but he led me to where it had once stood. We walked to the back of the hall and up a few steps and he pointed to the performance area and then the back door to the stage where The Beatles had brought their gear through, after getting it all out of their van. When I mentioned the incident that happened in the car park when the teddy boys had caused a fight, Brian wasn't that interested, so I said thanks for the guided tour and asked him if I could go out through the back door from the stage. "Sure," he said and came over to the door and unlocked it. I stepped down into the little car park at the side of the hall and spent a silent moment or two picturing where The Beatles' Commer van had been parked when they were loading their equipment back into it. Reaching into my pocket, I took out a guitar plectrum that I had and placed it on the spot where the van was probably parked the night they played Lathom Hall. As I walked back to my car and drove off I felt glad that I found the place but sad that the hall had been the setting for a vicious attack on the group that was partly responsible for Stuart Sutcliffe's haemorrhage. The incident also left John Lennon with an injured hand. I wanted to find out more about Stuart, especially where he was buried. From a video showing old footage of the early Beatles I discovered a ten second clip of his grave at the back of a cemetery. The clip was enough to help me establish the colour and shape of his headstone which I then tracked down as being in a cemetery in Hyton.

 I had to visit the cemetery to find out more about Stuart. After finding the church that Stuart attended, on Bluebell Lane in Hyton, I walked across the street to a little graveyard and without any problem I almost walked straight up to the headstone. Near the back of the cemetery Stuart's headstone was in polished black marble with Stuart and his dad's name etched in gold lettering. The grave hadn't been visited much judging by the jar on it containing two dead flowers. I swept a few of the dead leaves away from around the base of the headstone and felt that I wanted to do more. Strangely enough, the opportunity to do more did come years later when I was able to safely secure Stuart's gradually collapsing headstone for all to remember him.

Every time that I travelled to Liverpool I would go and pay my respects to Stuart and over the years I noticed that his headstone was leaning forward getting dangerously closer to the ground, year by year. My first thought was to contact the Sutcliffe family about the problem and although I tried I got nowhere. On the 22nd of June 2009, determined to do something, I contacted a stone mason to fix Stuart's headstone upright and secure it in the ground. That done, the following weekend I went up and touched in Stuart's name in gold lettering. Before leaving I tided the grave up and planted a flower that I'd picked from Strawberry Field years before. When first picked it I took it home and planted it in my garden. It seeded itself and grows all around my garden, back and front, and it has even found its way into the garden at Rochdale Fire station where I worked.

When planting the flower at Stuart's grave I left a plaque. Written on it were the words: "A flower has been planted here, taken from the field of strawberry." My hope was that it would bring him that little bit nearer to his best friend John, in the peaceful place where they both are now.

Eleanor Rigby's statue, dedicated to all the lonely people of Liverpool.

St. Barnabas Church at Penny Lane Roundabout.

The Fire Station on Mather Avenue.

The entrance to Allerton Golf Course and the path from John's to Paul's.

The old stone steps on John's side of the golf course leading onto the path that John and Paul took to reach each others homes.

St. Mary's Parish Church in Todmordon, where my search started.

Town Meadows in Rochdale, where Pablo Fanques Circus was performed in 1843.

13
The Beatlemania Plaque That Never Was
(Give it to me straight)

When I heard the news that Litherland Town Hall Ballroom was being converted into a walk in clinic, I was disappointed.

I called the Town Hall many times hoping that it would never come off. Litherland was where Beatlemania was born. The actual phrase may have been first used nationally a couple of years later but the first sign of real hysteria for the group began when The Beatles returned for the first time from Hamburg. Litherland was the first main venue that they played on the 27th of December 1960. The crowds went berserk that night and, unusually, they stopped dancing when The Beatles hit the stage wearing their all-leather gear and exploded into 'Long Tall Sally.' I can't be sure, but as a result of this show I seem to remember the word "Beatlemania" being printed in a newspaper in Liverpool at the time.

It was a sad day when I realised that it had all gone through for the hall to be changed into a walk in clinic when I called at the place in 2008. Wanting to take a look at what was going on, I was met with that much activity I couldn't get into the car park. Usually empty, this time it was full of builder's cabins and dozens of people walking about with hard hats on.

I walked up to the entrance to the ballroom and looked inside and was sickened to see that the old wooden ticket booth was gone and all that I could see was tons of scaffolding being erected. Sickened by this, I walked over to one of the cabins and asked could I go into the hall. The builder I had approached told me I couldn't for safety reasons then I asked what have you done with the old wooden ticket booth and he replied "ho we slung that out" I had to compose myself then I said that all I wanted to do now was to take some photos he told me to give him my camera and he would go inside the ballroom and take some for me. As this was the only way that I could get a last chance of seeing the hall I said thanks to the builder, glad that I'd caught it all on film years before. My thoughts wandered back to the day when David the security guy had shown How and me round and I'd videoed the stage and the changing room. Now it was all gone forever. Another iconic Beatles' location had been removed from the pop history map.

As it was an important fact that Beatlemania had been born at Litherland Hall, in July 2009 I contacted the now walk-in clinic and asked one of the secretaries if could I put a plaque up on the outside wall commemorating the place where Beatlemania was born. Having explained that I would be paying for the plaque and also paying for a firm to fit and mount it on the outside wall she said that they would look into it. Months and months went by and I was phoning the place every week. At last they said that they were having another board meeting and the plaque idea was brought up and discussed again.

Meanwhile, the manufacture of the plaque was underway. I'd called twice at a printing firm that was making the plaque for me to choose what type of wood should be used, what words and type of lettering and decide on the size of the highly polished brass plate. The printing firm was eager to make up the plaque when I told them where it was going to be mounted.

The people attending the board meeting asked for all the information about the plaque request to be put in writing. So I posted written details about what I was proposing and the suggested wording for the plaque. After their next meeting I phoned them and was told that it all looked promising so I started to get excited about the prospect of the Beatlemania plaque being reality.

The firm who were making the plaque were emailing me all the time asking me to let them know when I wanted to take delivery of the plaque. I passed on the good news to them telling them that all seemed to be going through now and that I was just waiting for the clinic to give me the final go-ahead. Then I faxed a letter to the clinic to tell them which wall the plaque was going on and how high up on the wall it was going to be fixed.

The process was going on that long that I believed I had a chance of the committee saying that the plaque could go up. Selling my pride and joy Sazuki acoustic guitar to Pat, who is one of the fire fighters at Rochdale, to help pay for the plaque, I also sent Paul McCartney a letter telling him that a plaque was going up.

Then in late November 2009 one of the secretaries emailed me telling me that at the last board meeting they had discussed the plaque being put on the outside wall and it was rejected because they didn't want Beatles tourists coming into the car park to see the plaque and clashing with patients who were coming to the clinic for treatment. I felt deflated because I'd been convinced that they would allow this important plaque to be put on the wall. After I'd thought about the decision for a while I could see their point in one respect but I couldn't help remembering that over the many years that I had visited the Litherland Town Hall Ballroom me and How were the only Beatles' fans turning up. Nobody else had shown any interest in the ballroom's dusty old stage and changing rooms.

14
The Door Opens To Aunt Mimi's
(I call your name)

John Halliday was still looking after Mendips when the National Trust asked one of John Lennon's cousins to look around the house and put them in the picture as to just what coloured carpets and furniture was in each room of the house when John Lennon lived there. The last owner, who'd passed away, had changed some of the carpets in the rooms.

Armed with the correct information about how the décor had changed when John's Aunt Mimi had moved out, they began the task of taking Mendips back to what it looked like when John lived there.

On a Sunday in March 2003 I called round to Forthlin Road to help John with the tours and while I was there he told me that all the work that had been going on at Mendips was now finished. The gardens and the interior of the house now looked the same as they had when John Lennon lived there all those decades ago. John told me that the tours of the property were now almost ready to start and that the National Trust had advertised for someone to be the custodian and live in the house. The interviews had taken place and they had found somebody for the job but they still needed another custodian on standby. The property tenure would then take over from the live-in custodian when he went on holiday or was taken sick. I asked John jokingly: "Are the wages a tenure an hour?" and he laughed.

That's when john put it to me – asking did I want the job? I was taken aback because this was something completely different to anything that I had done before. I was used to working in back street garages and a factory but not working right in the public's face. Even though I'd helped John out at Forthlin Road, talking to the tourists and answering questions about The Beatles, this time I would be on my own and totally in charge. It seemed to me to be too much for me to take on with no margin for error.

Encouragingly, John told me that I would be more than capable of doing the job because of my knowledge of The Beatles and John Lennon's childhood. He went on to praise the way I handled visitor questions that were asked at Forthlin Road. "Above all, Colin, you're trustworthy and that goes a long way," he said. I told him that doing the job would be living a dream for me but first I'd have to have a talk with Lynn when I got back home to see what she had to say.

On my return to Rochdale I told Lynn all about the job and that I would be living in the house all weekend sometimes away from home. Lynn was very understanding. She said that I always go that extra mile on anything that I become interested in, so with my passion for The Beatles I'd have to give it 100% and take the job. So it was settled and I told her that John Halliday would phone me in advance so that I could book a holiday off from work when Mendips needed looking after.

It was only a week later John phoned me and told me that the live in custodians at Mendips were going to have a weekend away and could I have time off work because one of the days fell on a Friday work day. I immediately agreed and booked the time off.

The dates of my first days at Mendips were on the 27th and 28th of May 2005. This weekend would turn out to be one of the most special and most nervous times of my life. The week leading up to that weekend seemed to skip along at work and I was thinking and worrying about my new role as the day approached. How would I do as the acting custodian? Finally the Friday arrived and I drove to Liverpool. After stopping for breakfast at Tesco I called on Forthlin Road to get the keys for Mendips.

I sat down and had a brew as John ran through everything I needed to do once again. That finished, he said that he would go with me to Mendips and see just how I did the job.

The tours always started with the bus driving from Speke Hall, where all the visitors got on, before unloading all the passengers in Menlove Avenue for the start of the hour-long tour of Mendips. Then the bus would return, after their hour was up, before driving each party of fans over to 20 Forthlin Road. Here they'd spend another hour in the McCartney's home. John said to me that he would stay with me until I'd finished that first tour and then he would hop on the tour bus and go back to Forthlin Road where he would do the second part of the tour showing them around the McCartney's home.

We finished our cup of tea before John said: "Right, let's go." On my short car journey to Mendips, I had to drive past the house and go right up the dual carriageway and then turn the car round to come back down the same road to park the car in a street opposite. My newish looking car wouldn't have looked right parked on the drive of Mendips, especially after the National Trust had taken a lot of time getting the house looking like it did when John lived there in the fifties and sixties.

After I had parked the car, John and me crossed over that dual carriageway and I watched Mendips getting closer and closer. I started to feel a bit nervous and my adrenalin was pumping.

When we got inside the house John unlocked the back kitchen door while I put my change of clothes and my shaving gear away and out of sight of the tourists. We checked right through the house to see that everything was in its place, then went outside and waited at the front gate for the first tour bus to arrive. For the last time, John went through everything I was to do, reminding me of the reasons why no photographs could be taken inside the house and that all tourists must be in the front room when I first talk to them. Just then John said in a quiet voice: "Here's the bus." Passing us on the other side of the dual carriageway, because it came from Speke Hall, it had to drive up to the traffic lights and turn round then drive back to us before pulling over at the grass verge.

The driver came round and opened the door of the bus and that's when I walked over and introduced myself before walking everyone in through the front gate of Mendips. After closing the gate I quickly did a head-count. I needed to make sure that no other person had slipped through because there were a number of other fans stood at the front gate taking photographs. John had already warned me about some people not officially on the tour occasionally taking the opportunity to slip in through the gate unnoticed. You had to be on your guard all the time.

I talked to the tourists at the gate telling them the story that John Halliday uses about Aunt Mimi never letting John Lennon's young friends in to the house through the front door. She insisted they always had to enter through the back door and I'd said the same thing. "I'm sure you're all John's friends - so, hey, we'll go in through the back door." The tourists always loved this and the remark generally got a laugh.

As we all got down to the bottom of the garden I pointed out the hedge telling the tourists that here was the hedge where John found a quicker route to get to Strawberry Field, the place where he used to play in his younger days. The tourists stood there for a few minutes in silence and just stared across the garden. Then I went round to the kitchen door, opened it and asked them inside. When they were all in the kitchen I told them the joke about this kitchen being the very first place that John got his O.B.E. (One Boiled Egg!). This got all the tourists laughing again and made things that bit more relaxed.

Ushering everyone into the living room I stood in the hallway with my back to the door, under the stairs, letting them all pass me. This was the point at which I had to ask them could they please let me have all cameras and any large bags that they had with them. These were to be locked up in the room under the stairs. That's when one gentleman, who was very reluctant to let me have his camera, kept on saying that his camera was a very expensive one and he wasn't happy about handing it over. I had to stress the point that I would take great care of all the cameras and belongings and that they would all be locked away in a safe place. Fortunately, in the end, he gave it to me.

With everyone now squeezed into the living room I welcomed them again to Mendips, the place where John Lennon used to live. Now I explained the reasons why I had to take their cameras and the ban on taking pictures of the photographs displayed around the walls of both Mendips and Forthlin Road. All the photos were rare and with no copyright permission. Mobile phones with built in cameras were also a problem, so I asked for those to be switched off and to be kept out of sight.

Then, after politely explaining all the rules, I started to talk about the time when John Lennon lived in Mendips with his Aunt Mimi and Uncle George along with paying residents from the veterinary college who would stay in the spare bedroom, providing Mimi with a little extra income. After I'd talked for a while I could see that they wanted to go and look around the house. Some of the group had travelled thousands of miles to take a look, so I finished the talk and told them that they could go in all the rooms except the back bedroom, the live-in custodian's bedroom and were free to go everywhere else in the house. As they headed off around the house I handed out laminated information guide sheets with written explanations of every room.

As I mingled with them, walking round the house and answering questions, I discovered that some of the people on the tour were from Argentina, there were a few from America and four Jewish people. They had all come together from different parts of the world with the same passion for seeing the houses that John Lennon and Paul McCartney grew up in.

While I walked round the house I noticed one lady looking at a photograph on the wall in the back room. The photograph was one of the early Beatles with Pete Best in the band and the lady turned to me and said that she was Pete Best's sister-in-law. "Just wait till I tell him that there's a photo on the wall in Mendips of him stood with George, John, Paul and Ringo," she said excitedly. She was so pleased that she had discovered Pete's picture on the wall at Mendips that I believed her story and was glad that she'd tell Pete about the photo. Being included in one of the pictures at The National Trust property was something I felt he should know.

When visiting time was nearly up I gave the group a shout, telling them that they had five minutes left in the house before the bus arrived. While most of them were waiting for me to give them their cameras and belongings back one of the Americans ran up the stairs to have a last look in John's bedroom. With the bus on its way to collect the group, I unlocked the door and handed them their cameras telling them they could now take photos in front of the house if they wanted to.

As the last visitor walked out of the house into the front garden I quickly went inside and ran round the house just checking that everything was still in its place and also counting the laminated sheet guides that were left all around the house. Everything was in order so I went outside and joined the group who were taking photographs. Some photographed me stood next to other members of the group while the rest stood near the gate waiting for the bus. As we had time I pointed out the lonely bus stop across the road which was the spot John Lennon's mother Julia was heading for on the day she was knocked down and killed by a motorist as she crossed over the dual carriageway.

Just then I caught sight of the bus driving up and asked the group if they'd enjoyed the visit and the stories I'd told them. They all appeared to have enjoyed every minute of it and from what they said it appeared that John's bedroom had been the high point. Calling out that I hoped to see them all again and wishing them a safe journey I waved to them as the bus set off for Forthlin Road with John Halliday sat in the front.

I walked back into the house and closed the door behind me. I brewed up and sat in the living room supping my tea. Everything was deadly silent now after thirteen people had been walking around the house just ten minutes ago. My first time alone in Mendips, it seemed so surreal me, sat there supping tea in the house where John Lennon lived.

But the house wasn't completely silent. The only sound was coming from John's bedroom. Here there was a tape recorder playing John's songs that was triggered when somebody walked into the bedroom. The tape recorder was behind the headboard of John's bed and the songs that were playing were that faint that you could only hear it when you entered the bedroom.

Putting my cup down, I walked up the stairs to John's bedroom and sat on his bed thinking that this was the room that John and Paul wrote 'Please Please Me'... 'Oh Yeah'. I went over to the window and I could see the stone steps on the pavement far up the road that led into the park where John and Paul used to go to get to each other's homes. I imagined John must have stood where I was standing watching out for Paul walking up the main road from the park with his guitar in his hand.

I had all the time in the world before the next tour so I walked all over the house looking in every room and stopped to stare at the photographs which were in the back room on show to the public. They pictured John when he was a little boy stranding at the front gate and in the back garden. Starting to feel hungry, I went downstairs and made some toast and another cup of tea, grabbed a chair and sat in the back garden, relaxing in the sun. Still nervy at the prospect of the second tour I worried mostly that someone on the tour would ask me a question and my answer wouldn't match the facts they'd read previously. So, I had it in my head to say that it just depended on which book you might have read. There must be a thousand books written about The Beatles, so some stories must differ.

When I'd finished my toast and tea, I had a walk round the back garden and stopped at the apple tree, bending down to pick up an apple that was lying in the grass. I wiped it on my jeans and then stuck my teeth into it and ate it. As I did so, I could just see John doing the same thing when he'd fancied an apple all those years ago. I went back to the house still eating the apple and got ready for the second tour.

Nearing the time for the second tour of the day I stood inside the front gate and after a minute or two the bus drove down Menlove Avenue. Full of tourists once more, it passed me on the other side of the road and some of the passengers looked across at me and I waved to them. As it turned around and stopped at the gate I opened the door to the bus and went through the same procedure as I'd done earlier in the day. More confidently this time, I asked them to switch off and hide their mobile phones. I didn't want to be in the middle of talking to them and someone's mobile phone ring out, answered excitedly by: "Guess where I am? I'm in John Lennon's bedroom!"

All went smoothly on the second tour until I went back into the house at the end of the tour to check round. Two of the laminated sheets were missing. Someone had taken them as a memento and I hadn't spotted who. I phoned John Halliday who was waiting for the same party of tourists to turn up at Forthlin Road and I told him about the two laminated sheets that had grown legs and to be on his guard. When I met up with John later in that day he said there were two men wearing long coats who never spoke a word and they started slipping off into different rooms on their own. Whether they were the culprits or not we'd never know but it was a good job that it was only the laminated sheets that were disappearing and not something valuable.

At the end of the first day, when I'd finished with the last tour, I went back inside Mendips and flopped on one of the chairs in the living room. I felt drained. It had been a long day and a busy one, answering so many questions from so many people but now it was so silent again. I began to nod off and I just stopped myself. Then I grabbed a chair and sat in the back garden with a can of lager. I felt I'd disserved it and started singing Beatles songs to myself, absolutely buzzing with excitement, knowing that I was going to sleep in John Lennon's aunt Mimi's house that night and somebody always had to be living on the premises for security reasons.

After I'd finished that can of lager, I walked back into the house and started to tidy and Hoover up to be ready for the first tour in the morning.

When the night drew in I remembered that my car was on the other side of the road where I'd parked it, so I drove it back over the road then parked it on Mendips' drive and closed the gates for the night. There was nothing to do all night and no television in the house. All that I could do all night was play some tapes that I had brought with me of songs I'd picked and play my guitar which I'd also brought with me. It felt strange playing songs in John Lennon's front room that John had written and sung but had never sung in Mendips.

Putting the guitar down, I wandered around the house looking at photographs and revisiting every room in silence before returning to the living room. Picking up my guitar again I strummed a few songs. After a while I tired of that but as I was putting the guitar back in its case a strange idea hit me. It would be the ultimate John Lennon tribute for me to do and unique in so far as nobody else could ever have done it. I would play and sing the song 'Imagine' while walking up the stairs and into John's bedroom. So I stood up and began to play and sing the song. I walked into the cold hallway and started to walk up the stairs and as I got to the top of the stairs and down the landing I started to hear a faint sound as I walked into John's bedroom. It was the tape recorder, and the song that was being played was 'Imagine', perfectly in time note for note. Stopping playing and singing, I put down my guitar and sat on his bed and said: "Carry on John. This is your song." As the recording finished I got a bit emotional and sat at the end of his bed as the tape recorder switched itself off. I knew then that John was with me in that room and I'll never forget it. It's true that your mind is a very strong thing and if you want something to happen it will happen and I wanted John to be there with me and he was. I could feel him with me in the house.

By this time I was ready for bed, so I went downstairs, locked up, turned the lights out and went back upstairs for a wash. Then I jumped into bed and before I turned over I whispered: "Goodnight John." and then first thing in the morning I'd say: "Good morning John."

15
Sgt. Pepper Arrives At Mendips
(Uninvited)

The day after my first stint as custodian at Mendips I decided to start the day with a bath. Then it was downstairs for three rounds of toast with jam. I'd brought jam for breakfast and some scotch eggs and meat pies for my dinner and tea.

When I'd finished breakfast I started to clear up and I heard a buzzing sound and noticed a bee flying round the kitchen. It was a big thing and I thought I'd better get rid of it. Tourists visit the kitchen and I didn't want them ducking and weaving trying to get out of the way of the bee while I'm trying to talk to them. So, determined to get the bee out of the kitchen, I opened the kitchen door and picked up the tea towel and started wafting away at the bee, trying my best to coax it out through the kitchen door. While doing this I hadn't noticed the light fitting which hung down on a thin wire from the ceiling. On the light fitting was a glass shade. As I took a swipe at the bee the tea towel hit the shade and smashed it against the ceiling. The bee then had the cheek to fly out through the kitchen door and I stood there with broken glass all around me on the floor. I looked at the clock and realised the first tour was arriving in ten minutes. All the blood drained from me. Searching frantically for a brush and shovel, I found what I was looking for and then swept the broken glass up and put it into a plastic bag. Then I clambered up on a chair from the dining room and used it to stand on while I unscrewed and removed the broken shade that was left hanging on the end of the wire. Now all that was left hanging from the ceiling was a wire with a 60 watt bulb at the end of it. No doubt the tourists spotted this and maybe thought that Mimi's standard of living must have been poor. The late fifties-style shade was very swiftly replaced with a spare one that the National Trust had in stock.

Everything was done and dusted in the house ready for the first tour of day two and after greeting the group of tourists at the gate and talking to them in the living room I found out that some were from Yorkshire some from Liverpool itself and there were seven that had travelled all the way from Canada. It did seem strange telling stories about John Lennon and The Beatles to people that lived in Liverpool and me coming from Rochdale. The locals from Liverpool told me about them knowing John Lennon at school and there was one lady whose sister had gone out with him. I wanted to talk with her some more but I had to mingle with the rest of the group. Whenever I was in the back room with the tourists I would always point out the Stuart Sutcliffe photograph and tell them that after his tragic death in Hamburg his family brought his body back and had him buried in Hyton Cemetery, about eight miles from where we were standing. I was always amazed at how many people didn't know that his body was brought back to the UK and buried here.

The day seemed long again and after I'd shown the last tour around the house I did the last tidying up before packing up all my stuff. After locking the house up I drove to Forthlin Road to give the keys back to John Halliday.

Back at Forthlin Road John and I sat and talked about how I'd managed with the tours that weekend. I told John what a privilege it had been to stay in Mendips and how whenever I was waiting for the next tourist bus to turn up there was always somebody out there taking photographs or just stood there speechless staring at the house. Many times interested people asked if I could let them in to have a look around. Sadly I had to turn them all away. Everyone who wanted to visit Mendips had to book a tour to see inside both John and Paul's houses.

After I had a good natter with John I couldn't wait to get home and tell everybody what I'd done that weekend.

About a month later I got a phone call from John asking if I was free to come over to Liverpool that Thursday. The day was the 9th of June and I said I'd happily book a single day's holiday off at work. He explained that Mr and Mrs Colin Hall, the custodians at Mendips, were having a day off and would I fill in for them. I couldn't wait for that Thursday to come round. My excitement was increased by the fact that I'd made up a special suit to wear while showing the tourists round. My outfit would be a copy of The Beatles Sgt. Peppers uniform made up of a black jacket with silver buttons and medals, black trousers and topped off with a big white moustache with a uniform cap stuck on my head.

This was the uniform that the conductor of the Sgt. Peppers band wore in the film Yellow Submarine. The conductor was in fact Sgt. Pepper himself, so I couldn't wait to see John Halliday's face when I turned up wearing this garb. When the day arrived I set off down the M62 at 6.30 in the morning all dressed up in my Sgt. Peppers uniform but minus my hat and moustache. Turning off the motorway at junction 12, I drove past Brian Epstein's family home on Queen's Drive. It suddenly dawned on me that I was too early to get a breakfast at Tesco's (not Tiffany's!) so I had some time to kill and decided to drive into the back yard of Penny Lane fire station .

When I parked the car up in their yard I attached my false moustache under my nose and put on my hat. Getting out of the car I walked into the back of the station where the fire fighters were washing down the pump. Even though I was dressed up like a dog's dinner with a big white funny moustache, they just looked up and said in there typical calm Liverpool voices: "Morning mate!"

I told them that I worked at Rochdale fire station and showed them my ID while explaining I had a day off. I went on to tell them about my job showing tourists round John Lennon's former home and the reason why I was dressed up in my Sgt. Pepper uniform at such an early time in the morning. They pointed to the staircase and told me to go and get a brew. So, I went tripping up the stairs. I knew where everywhere was because I'd been inside the station before, although not in these clothes. Walking through the locker room and passing the pool table I entered the mess where one lad spotted me and started laughing. Then two others that were in the kitchen were set off laughing too. They asked me why I was dressed as I was and while I sat down they made me a cup of coffee before sitting down with me while I told them about my passion over the years for finding out where The Beatles grew up in Liverpool and the places in their songs like Penny Lane fire station.

By this time I could see that they were getting ready to stand down and change over watches, so I said thanks for the coffee and walked back through the station's engine house where some of the watch were getting ready to change over the shift. It's usual for an army style line-up with polished shoes and everyone stood to attention when there's a changeover but when they all saw me with my big piece of fur stuck under my nose they all burst out laughing again. I smiled at them all, walked through to the back yard and got back in my car and drove to Tesco's which was just over the Road from the station.

I wanted to see the public's reaction to me being dressed up in my uniform. In another few hours I'd be showing tourists round Mendips for the first time dressed as Sgt. Pepper. So, as a test, I put my hat on (I already had my moustache stuck under my nose), got out of my car and marched through to the café. After picking what I wanted to eat I sat down and started my breakfast. Nobody seemed to be that bothered with the way I was dressed! Then I did a bit of shopping to get some stuff for my dinner. A lot of people stared and some smiled at me. I was only too glad it was the women who smiled and not the men! After I had bought some food I drove to Forthlin Road and knocked on the door. When John opened the door and saw how I was dressed he didn't seem very amused! It wasn't until months and months later that John told me that The National Trust bosses simply wanted their custodians to wear normal everyday clothes. Even after hearing this I carried on putting the jacket, moustache and hat on. It didn't feel out of the ordinary to me because after all it was a uniform. The silver-buttoned black blazer, polished shoes and cap all fitted the job. I suppose I had to admit though that the big white moustache stuck under my nose did look a bit odd!

After I'd picked up the keys from John for Mendips I went round to the house and let myself in, unlocking the kitchen door as usual. Once I'd checked all around I sat down nervously waiting for the first tour to arrive. When it got near the time I stood at the front gate and when the bus eventually pulled up I did my usual job of explaining about the cameras and phones. Everyone appeared to be delighted to see me dressed as Sgt. Pepper and at the end of the tour, when given their cameras back, they all wanted photographs of me standing with them in the front garden. I have never had my photograph taken so many times.

At each tour all the comments were the same. The uniform had made their visit more fun, they said. As the last tour of the day ended I went back into the house and flumped onto a chair in the cold front room again. Then something odd happened. Sitting there in peace and quiet after the long day I found myself looking around the room and after a while I realised that the furniture in the room that I was looking at was at a different angle from the place from where I was sat. The place from where I was looking was behind me above the bay window that was at the back of me, up near the ceiling. Next, unbelievably, I was looking at myself from behind me. In my mind I thought: "It's not me sitting in this room," and then realised that I was having an out-of-body experience.

During my out-of-body experience my eyes seemed to float around the room and it always seemed to involve me looking from above, up against the ceiling. I say "always" as I'd had this feeling a few times before. Previously this had happened to me back home, possibly because, at that time, I had been practicing Tibetan Buddhism. It was something I had been doing for 13 years, which involved a lot of meditating over that period.

After I had a rest and recovered from my out-of-body experience I tided up the house got my things together and had a last look in John's bedroom before locking the house up. I drove to Forthlin Road and gave the keys back to John Halliday. When he asked me how the day's tours had gone I told him how the tourists loved the way that I'd dressed up as Sgt. Pepper - especially the Americans. I didn't bother telling him about the experience I'd had in the living room. I didn't want him to think that I was odd as it's the sort of thing that's difficult to describe without frightening people. However, I told a couple of friends about the out-of-body experience when I got back home and I just felt I had to include the experience in this book.

16
The Strawberry Field Gates Are Vandalised
(I'll get the paint out)

Between the custodian jobs at Mendips, I'd still go up to Liverpool and visit Beatles' locations. Driving past Strawberry Field main gates regularly over the years I noticed that they weren't being looked after and, worse still, they were now being vandalised.

Small parts of the cast iron gates had been removed and the grounds, just at the back of the gates, were overgrown. There was litter and tons of old leaves swept up to the front of the gates. They looked a mess. So I reported the vandalism to the police at the police station on Calderstone Road and they said that they would make a note to put the gates on Beaconsfield Road on their route at night.

On 29th of February 2007 I got in touch with Liverpool town hall and asked a guy who sounded very young and he gave me a phone number to ring and when I rang it, it turned out to be Wigan rugby club, he got it mixed up" I think" I kept on phoning the town hall and finally got in touch with someone who could help me so I asked him if I could put a conservation order on the Strawberry Field gates. The reply came back that I couldn't just put an order on the gates and I would have to put one on the building inside the grounds and the wall surrounding the building. This was getting too much for me, so I sent two letters to two important people who are connected with The Beatles. Unfortunately I got no reply. I don't even know if they got the letters. People like them seem to employ others to read through all their mail first, binning letters like mine. All my concern for these gates seemed to be falling on deaf ears.

But I couldn't let the condition of the Strawberry Field gates get any worse. So, I decided to do something about the state of the gates and see if I could get permission to clean the area up and paint the gates myself. At least that way I might make it look like somebody was still in charge of the precious gates and they weren't just left for anybody to take bits off.

So, after finding the telephone number for the Captain at the Salvation Army headquarters, I phoned him and asked him would he please give me permission to paint Strawberry Field gates and told him the reason why. When he said he didn't see why not, I couldn't believe my ears! Before putting the phone down I asked him to please put what he had told me in writing, just in case the police were to stop me and ask who'd given me permission to paint the gates.

The Captain promised that he would put in writing what he'd told me and true to his word, three days later I got the letter giving me permission. That letter from Salvation Army HQ would eventually end up framed and hung on the wall at home, alongside the paint brushes that I used to paint the Strawberry Field gates.

With the letter giving me permission to paint the gates safely in my possession, I went looking for a tin of bright red paint. I looked on an old video that I took years ago to research the right colour red and decided to make the trip to Liverpool to do the job on the following Saturday.

It was a hot sunny day on Saturday the 18th of April 2009 when I set out for work at Strawberry Field. When I arrived, I drove right into the grounds of Strawberry Field, then walked round to the main gates and set up safety signs and cones with barrier tape. Then I returned to the car for a shovel, sweeping brush, ladders, tins of paint and paint brushes. I put my overhauls on and started to try and remove some of the graffiti on the stone pillars using a wire brush and paint stripper. Next, I climbed over the gates and cut back the overgrown bushes and swept up the tons of leaves, litter and broken branches. The clear-up took ages but when I'd finished, I climbed back over the gates and then rubbed them down using my wire brush. Then I flipped the lid off one of the tins of paint. The bright red paint gleamed at me as I stuck my brush into it and started to paint. While I was painting there were people passing by all day long and every one of them stopped and asked why I was doing what I was doing and not somebody from the authorities in Liverpool. They were surprised when I explained the situation but I didn't have much time for conversation, I had a lot of cast iron to paint. All the people passing the gates that day were glad to see the gates being painted and they told me so.

I carried on painting thinking to myself that Beaconsfield Road (where Strawberry Field is situated) seemed to be quiet for a Saturday. But, the quiet wasn't to last long. Just then a full-size coach drove onto the very narrow pavement right next to my ladders. It must have been a 60-seater coach.

Well, everybody piled off the coach onto the narrow pavement in front of the gates where I was painting and the coach driver came over to me and told me what a good job I was doing. He went on to explain that he brought tours every day to see the gates and he felt embarrassed about the state of them and the way they were looking. He was glad to see someone was doing something about it.

As I listened to the tourists chattering I realised that most of them were Americans, two of whom were interested in buying my paint brushes! I told them that I couldn't as I was still using the brushes, otherwise I would have gladly done so. One of the Americans, who took a photograph with me holding up one of the tins of red paint, wanted to shake my hand and when I drew his attention to the paint on my hand he said: "That's one of the reasons why I wanted to shake your hand so I could get some of that red paint on my hand!" I told him that if he waited a couple of hours he could have all the empty tins and he just laughed.

Then I spotted another two lads who were about 19 or 20. They were getting closer to my wet paint and when I warned them not to get too close one of them took off his jacket. For I moment I thought the lad meant trouble until he asked if he could get a bit closer so he could lean on the freshly painted red gates and get the pattern of the gates onto his white T-shirt. I couldn't believe what I was hearing! I warned him that if he did and returned to sit down on the coach there would be paint all over the back of the seat. I could see the lad milling it over in his mind but then he put his jacket back on and got back among the crowd that had got off the coach.

Standing back to let the tourists take their last photos I then waved them off with my paint brushes. That was the first coach to turn up at the gates that day but it wasn't the last. Another three followed and there must have been seven taxis during the rest of the day pulling up onto the pavement to show their taxi fares the famous gates. I could have sold those paint brushes 60 times over - the amount of people that wanted them was mind-blowing.

I was having difficulty carrying on with my painting with all the interruptions but I was glad to see so many people coming from all over the world and still wanting to see the gates.

Feeling a bit hungry, I left all my gear at the gates and walked back to my car to grab a sandwich and a drink. While I was sat in the car, I gazed across the grounds to where the old orphanage used to be and noticed some old stone steps in the middle of a field. They were the stone steps that I remembered I had seen before in an old photograph I had at home of the Victorian orphanage. Those stone steps lay in front of the old building which has now long since gone.

When I finished my sandwich, I walked over to the steps and took some photographs and while I was taking several pictures I disturbed a fox that was lying in the long grass which ran off in the direction of Mendips.

Later, when I had those photos developed they didn't' quite capture the feeling that I had for the place. Photographs can only record so much, I suppose. After taking my pictures I walked back to the gates and carried on painting and, in between all the taxis and coaches pulling up, a car mounted the pavement, stopped and a young bloke got out. Walking over to me he said he was from Channel M Television and could he film me and do an interview. When I agreed, he rigged his camera equipment up and told me not to move out of the camera's vision and then to start talking. So I told the story about me getting permission to paint the gates and how John Lennon immortalised Strawberry Field because he played there as a child and ended up writing the famous song 'Strawberry Fields Forever '.

When he'd stopped filming the bloke said he was happy with what he'd got and he gave me his card. While he was packing up his equipment he asked me to give him a call if I decided to do anything else around Liverpool.

I spent another few hours painting and finishing off after the TV bloke had gone but I started feeling whacked. I'd been there for eight hours with the baking hot sun on my back, so I tided up and put everything back in my car, took my overhauls off and threw them in the back seat, before taking a last look at the lovely grounds of Strawberry Field. Then I drove out of the top gate and motored past the freshly painted gates, thinking that it was worth all the time and trouble I'd spent.

When I got home all the family had watched me on Channel M painting the gates. I felt famous for a day especially after three radio channels interviewed me over the air a few days later while I was at work. My week was complete when Gary Ashton, one of the fire fighters at the station, handed me a water colour picture he'd painted for me of Strawberry Field.

Then my fame spread on the internet. When I went online I had a few questions mainly asking why I painted the gates and not someone from Liverpool. All I could say was that I must have been more concerned than anybody else about the condition of the gates. Then I got an email telling me that I'd painted the gates the wrong colour! I thought whoever sent the email must be on something, so I didn't answer that one! When I called on Forthlin Road a week later to help John out, he told me that I was in all the papers and everyone was talking about this chap from Rochdale travelling up to Liverpool just to paint Strawberry Field gates. I felt like the bees knees when he told me this and when the tours started to arrive and I took the cameras and baggage off the tourists John introduced me as the custodian that stands-in at John Lennon's aunt Mimi's house and the man who painted Strawberry Field gates last week. "If there is anything that you want to know about

The Beatles, just ask Colin" he added. My face was as red as Strawberry Field gates.

A few years later the old gates were removed and a brand new pair fitted. So now, the current gates are not the original Strawberry Field gates that I painted. I will never understand why they were changed. These days when I visit and look at the gates I get the feeling that the soul has been removed from this famous field. Because They are not the gates that John Lennon as a kid once climbed over to loose himself in his magical garden.

17
The Living Dream
(I got the job)

Working at Mendips had really increased my passion for The Beatles. A couple of weeks after my last weekend's work there I drove up to Liverpool and called into Forthlin Road to see John Halliday. It was on a Saturday and we decided, because it was early, we would take Molly for a walk in Calderstone Park.

When we were leaving the house, John said he had something to ask me. We both got into the car with Molly and I said: "Come on John, hit me with it. What is it?" It turned out that he was going into hospital for a minor eye operation and he asked if I would help him out and be the custodian at Forthlin Road. He didn't want to get anybody else in to do the job. I'd been in the house more than anybody else and heard John give tourist talks in all the rooms and I knew all the McCartney family history. All that and my experiences as custodian at Mendips stood me in good stead, he said if I'd take over. He went on to explain that it might be for just one or two days and that I could sleep in Paul's bedroom, which I'd done many times before.

I readily agreed, as he continued to map out the plan for covering for him in a fortnight's time. When he began to tell me what my pay would be, I cut in saying: "I don't want paying, John. I'll be doing it to help you out. I don't want the money." But he explained that the National Trust had already begun sorting the payment out for me.

The two weeks flew by and on my first day covering for John at the McCartney's home I parked my car in a side street to avoid it getting in the way of the tourist traffic in Forthlin Road. It was a narrow road attracting dozens and dozens of tourist's who would stand on the pavement taking photos all day long.

I walked down the path to the front door of No.20 and lifted the letterbox shutter and started singing "Molly my dear". It was my version of the song that Paul McCartney wrote for his dog ("Martha my dear"), so I always sang it to Molly when I knocked on the door. When she heard my voice she'd always start running up and down the lobby crying, but she always knew it was me at the front door and she was always glad to see me.

When John opened the door he looked in no fit state to do anything. He'd had his operation and he said to me that he would keep in the back ground and might even go up to bed while I'm doing the tour and get his head down.

It was time for the first tour to start so when the bus pulled up I was ready to meet everyone at the front gate. The times had changed now and we no longer met the bus at the top of the street. It now drove down the street and stopped at the front door of Forthlin Road.

I walked up to the door of the bus and introduced myself as usual and led the group down the path and in through the front door before taking their cameras and belongings off them and talking to them in the living room. The talk seemed to go so smoothly and talking about the McCartney family living there was made easy by the photos on the walls almost telling the story's for me.

Then I explained that the living room where they were all standing was the place where John and Paul wrote over 100 songs and Mike McCartney had captured those moments snapping John and Paul in the room practicing with their guitars. Songs they wrote at Forthlin Road included 'Love Me Do', 'I Saw Her Standing There' and at least two family songs, which Paul wrote later, recalling times at home with his parents: 'When I'm Sixty Four' written for his father and 'Let It Be' all about his mother. As we were all looking at the pictures I took the opportunity to point out the patterned wallpaper on the back wall. It was noticeable that as one patterned wallpaper ended, another (different) patterned wallpaper began and I explained that this was because Dad Jim had run out of the paper that he started with so he used some spare rolls that he found. This always made the tourists laugh. Then we all headed for the dining room where there were more photos and some Beatles' memorabilia to look at.

After they had been in the dining room for about five minutes looking around I pointed out an old Bakelite phone which was mounted on the wall. I told them that the neighbours must have thought that the McCartney family were posh because they had a telephone and were probably the only ones in the street to have one. The reason they had a phone all those years ago was simple. Mother Mary was a mid- wife and she needed it for her job. Next I told them the funny story that John Halliday had told me about the Bakelite telephone. In the centre of the dial there's a piece of paper and on it is the phone number. So, back in the 60s that was Paul McCartney's telephone number. The lady who had been standing next to John said loudly: "Well that's no good to me now, is it!"

After the group had stopped laughing at the telephone story I walked them through to the kitchen and then into the back garden where I showed them the drainpipe that Paul used to climb up to get into the house and let his mate John Lennon in. Then I'd point out the outside toilet connected to an outhouse where Paul and Michael McCartney used to lie on top of the roof and watch the police training with their horses at the police training ground, which they could see just over their garden hedge.

Then when the tourists had finished looking at nearly every single plant in the back garden I beckoned them inside to show off the bedrooms. They had a good giggle at Mike McCartney's photo of his Dad washing socks and then we all went up the stairs to Paul's bedroom on the left at the top. It is that small I couldn't get all the tourists in the bedroom so some had to wait outside on the landing. There wasn't much to see anyway because there was only a small bed, a chair and a small bedroom cabinet and two photographs on the wall of Paul.

There was a dresser in Mike McCartney's back bedroom and a wardrobe which I showed them and that about ended the tour. I told them that they had five more minutes left to look around before the bus arrived and some stayed upstairs and some went downstairs and into the living room. I went downstairs and unlocked the room where I kept the tourists' cameras ready to give them back. As the bus parked up in the road I returned their property telling everyone that they could now take pictures in the front garden before leaving. When they had taken enough snaps they got back on the bus and I waved them off as it drove away to Speke Hall.

The next three tours went smoothly and John Halliday, who had stayed in the background all the time, told me that I'd done a good job. I was chuffed to hear that because I didn't have any idea just how my presentation had gone down with the tourists.

After that busy day John and I took Molly for a walk and while we were out we bought some food to take back. I went upstairs and brought down Johns old 12-inch television. It was that old I'm sure that if he'd left it in the living room on show the tourists would have thought it was the one that the McCartney's owned. We ate the food that we had brought in and watched some television. After a while I could see John was looking a bit weary. The operation from the day before was beginning to take its toll on him. I felt a bit tired myself, so I went into the kitchen, washed the few pots that were there and then said I was going to bed.

Even though I'd slept in Paul's bedroom eight times before, I still couldn't wait to get into that bed again. It was a living dream looking out of that little bedroom window, seeing the garden hedge that I had stood on the other side of so many times over the years, standing there looking up at Paul's bedroom wondering just what it looked like on the other side. Now it had become a living dream living in John and Paul's old homes, two of The Beatles that I hadn't been able to see 40 years before in that little coffee bar in a back street in Manchester.

After a shower, I jumped into bed and before I nodded off I lay their looking around the room wondering just where Paul had got his inspiration from to write over 100 songs in the house. Well, I thought, it certainly wasn't from this bedroom! He was born a natural musical genius. Meeting up with John,

George and Ringo, it was like it was set in stone that they would become the biggest band in the world.

18
John Lost His Job And I Lost Mine
(So I'll be on my way)

There came a time when I was no longer asked to show tourists round John Lennon's childhood home. Whether it was because I used to dress up as Sgt. Pepper and it didn't go down well with the people that run the National Trust or because I had an accident with that lamp shade and the bee in the kitchen at Mendips I don't know. But, I still carried on helping John out at Forthlin Road until sadly one day, while John was showing the tourists around the McCartney's house, one of them reported back to head office that they could smell beer on John's breath. So, after doing that job for 11 years as the custodian and living in that house (which was longer than the McCartney family did), John lost his job.

When I heard about this on the news I travelled up to Liverpool to find out where John was living. Knowing that he had no family to put him up and no money, I called in shops that he used to go in and knocked on doors all over the place until one of his neighbours told me that he was living in a back street in Allerton. The neighbour didn't know the address but thought it was near to some shops, where John was living with a friend who had kindly put him up. I drove up and down the streets and finally got out of my car and started walking and knocking on doors. As luck would have it, I turned a corner near some shops and I spotted John with Molly crossing the street. Walking up alongside him, he turned to me and said: "Hi Col. How did you find me?" "It's a long story!" I replied.

John looked down and out. I walked round the streets with him and Molly for a while talking about losing his job. When we got back to his friend's house he said: "Come in and have a brew." So I walked in and sat on the couch, still talking to John, who sat on one of the chairs staring at the floor. I tried to cheer him up, telling him that people from all over the world that I've heard from on the internet have said his tours of Forthlin Road were the best. He'd been acknowledged as the best ever custodian to have that job and that his warm humour would be missed. This did buck him up a bit because he was unaware that so many people from different parts of the world were asking why he'd lost his job.

Seeing him sat there in the state he was in, when two months before he was living in Forthlin Road, longer than the McCartney's had, showing people round in a steady job, I realised it was no longer to be. I chatted for an hour or two, then got up and said I'd better get going. That's when John reached over and got a newspaper out of a drawer. It was the Liverpool Echo and the headline read: "GUIDE GETS THE BOOT" and the article underneath was all about John losing his job. John started to write something at the top of the newspaper. Then he gave it to me and said: "You can have that." I looked at what John had written and it read: "To Colin: You are a true friend, you made it your business to look for me. With friends like you I will get by - John Halliday." I took the paper and as I'm writing this, it is in front of me on the table.

I said goodbye at the front door and felt so sorry for him. All that he seemed to have were the clothes on his back, so I gave him some money and told him that I would keep in touch. I've been a couple of times since then and gave him some things but he still looks the worse for wear.

I reminded him of something that he'd told me many years ago, that when problems crop up in your life, just keep on going and you'll reach the other side. Don't give up.

After I visit John I still (after twenty years) drive around the sights in Liverpool and even though most of them just seem like ordinary places that are hidden in the back streets, they still draw thousands and thousands of people from all over the world to come and see the places that four local lads have made iconic. I still get butterflies in my stomach when I drive to these places, even after losing my job working for the National trust. I can't stop reminiscing about the unforgettable times that I had in Liverpool, living in the houses where John and Paul spent their younger years, before and after they met, to become the biggest band ever.

All the locations I discover while walking the back streets of Liverpool are like a magical spell for me. When I get close to them I still get a buzz knowing what's around the corner and most of all knowing the story behind those special places that will never, ever stop singing to me.

THE END

This book is also available on Amazon as an eBook: search for 'I've Just Seen A Place I Can't Forget'.

The unofficial Beatles Liverpool App can be found on iTunes.

For more stories, please visit www.beatlemaniac.co.uk

The back of Strawberry Field gates with Colin's step ladder and sweeping brushes.

Printed in Great Britain
by Amazon